knitting pretty

○
○
○

knittingpretty

simple instructions for 30 fabulous projects

by kris percival

photographs by france ruffenach

CHRONICLE BOOKS
SAN FRANCISCO

o o o

Text copyright © 2002 by Kris Percival
Photographs copyright © 2002 by France Ruffenach
Illustrations copyright © 2002 by Randi Katzman

Library of Congress Cataloging-in-Publication Data available.

ISBN: 0-8118-3533-2

Manufactured in China.

Designed by Efrat Rafaeli
Illustrations by Randi Katzman, Creative Freelancers
Styling by Aaron Hom, Zenobia

Distributed in Canada by
Raincoast Books
9050 Shaughnessy Street
Vancouver, British Columbia V6P 6E5

10 9 8 7

Chronicle Books LLC
85 Second Street
San Francisco, California 94105
www.chroniclebooks.com

o o o

o   o   o

Many thanks to knitters and nonknitters—your advice, help, and support
was invaluable: Rebecca, Kathy, Dad, Penny, Keith, Chris Lee, Nicole and the
rest of the Brooklyn pals, Aunt Linda, Morgan, Bernhard, and Mikyla, Jodi,
and Beth at Chronicle.

This book is dedicated to Doron, Mom, and Aunt Babe.

o   o   o

table of contents

introduction

○ ○ ○

Have you noticed that hand-knit sweaters, scarves, mittens, and hats feel cozier and softer than store-bought items?

For centuries, hand-made knits have warmed the hands, the feet, and the veritable cockles of the heart. Mothers have long passed the craft of knitting on to their daughters, and their daughters have passed it to their daughters. At times, men too have gotten into the act. In earlier seafaring days, sailors commonly took yarn and needles to sea and knit away below-decks. It has only been in the past century, with the availability of mass-produced knits, that the art of knitting has fallen out of general knowledge. What once used to be a skill as common and necessary as cooking is now a soothing diversion and a comforting connection to days gone by.

Today, you can walk into any clothing store and find beautiful knit scarves and sweaters—all ready for you to purchase and wear. So the question is, why knit? The answer is simple: Knitting is fun. From the first trip to the yarn store, where shelves are piled high with soft fibers of every color and texture, to the stolen moments of peace when a knitter loses herself in the soothing rhythms of the work, knitting is a creative, meditative, and calming pursuit. Each knitter brings her own sense of color and style to the process, and the finished pieces are made that much warmer by the knitter's hands.

Perhaps you have admired others' knits from the sidelines, or maybe you're a confirmed knitter in search of new ideas to get your well-worn needles clacking. In **Knitting Pretty**, we've taken pains to offer knitting projects that are as accessible as they are enjoyable. The "Getting Started" chapter gives an overview of the simple materials needed—yarn, needles, and other accou- trements. In "How to Knit" you'll find simple, straightforward instructions for all the techniques you'll need to know to complete the projects in this book.

With these basics under your belt, you'll be ready to move on to the projects. All directions are written in plain English—you won't need to wrestle with the complicated abbreviations that have scared off more than one beginner. I've also rated the difficulty of each project on a scale of 1 to 5, so you'll know what you're getting into. At the beginning of each project, you'll find a complete list of all the materials needed, as well as the techniques necessary to complete that particular project. If you want to duplicate the item exactly as shown in the photograph, you can turn to the "Yarns Used for Projects" list (page 117), and the "Resources" section at the back of the book will get you started in your search for yarn, tools, and patterns.

To make things even clearer, the projects are divided into six chapters. "First Projects" is for true beginners and offers straightforward projects like a simple bookmark. "Old Favorites" features snuggly stand-bys that fit every winter need, such as a super-long ribbed scarf and a pair of warm mittens. From there it's on to "Adorable Knits for Kids of All Ages," where you can learn how to make silly clothes for sock puppets or a sassy tube top. "Modern-Day Accoutrements" features a few of the must-haves of modern life, such as a cell phone cozy and a hipster kerchief. Turn to "Creative Home Decor" to add some glad to your pad. Whip up a colorful pillow cover, or make a paperweight for your desk. Finally, "Tops of All Types" includes all the information you need to make a swishy, swinging poncho or a simple, cozy sweater.

The patterns in these pages are projects in their own right, but each is also only a starting point for your own ideas. Feel free to improvise as you go. You can make the same project many times, always with a different end result. Let yourself experience the joy, creativity, and color of knitting. Grab some needles and yarn, and let's get started!

getting
started

Because knitting comes with its own set of tools and terms, it's easy to feel intimidated at first. Before you knit a stitch, consider preliminary matters such as choosing and preparing yarn, the materials you'll need to have on hand, and a few basic concepts behind knitting. In this chapter you'll find a simple guide to familiarize you with the terms and tools you'll need as you embark on your knitting adventures.

yarns

Who knew that there were so many different kinds of yarn? Here are a few things to keep in mind when making your selection.

color

One of the best things about yarn is that it's available in so many colors. Most yarns are dyed in solid colors, but you may also want to look for tweeds, which feature different-colored flecks, and variegated yarns, which contain lengths of different colors. These yarns lend a rich and complex look to a beginner project.

dye lots

You may notice that acrylics and some wool have "no dye lot" written on their labels. This means that the yarn color won't vary from batch to batch. With most wools, however, it's best to buy more yarn than you think you'll need for a project, as dye lots tend to be small and extremely difficult to match. If you run out before finishing a project and go back to the store for more, you may not find a precise match. The most important thing is to choose a yarn you love. Touch it, gaze at it, even smell it—you and your yarn will be spending a lot of time together.

fiber type

I encourage absolute beginners to knit first with acrylic, a synthetic fiber that doesn't fray or separate as easily as wool. Acrylic is cheap and readily available at larger drugstores as well as yarn shops, and it comes in a wide range of colors. Once you become comfortable with the basic operations of the craft, you can move on to knitting with wool and other types of yarns such as cotton, alpaca (from llamas), and mohair (from goats).

skeins and balls

Some yarns come in skeins that you need to wind by hand into a ball. To do this, untwist the skein and ask a friend to hold the open skein snugly over her hands while you wind. You can use the back of a chair or even your feet if you don't have a friend handy. Eventually, you may want to invest in a *swift* and a *ball winder,* which are tools that considerably hasten the winding process. Many brands of yarn, and most acrylics, are wound into a *pull skein* that allows you to begin knitting immediately. When in doubt, ask your friendly yarn purveyor if you'll need to wind that yarn into a ball.

texture

For beginners, I recommend traditionally spun yarns without bumps, fuzz, or elastic. However, as you gain skill and confidence, you're likely to want to experiment with yarns of differing texture and weight. Several specialty yarns are available, including nubbly *bouclé,* fuzzy mohair, finely spun linen and silk, and plush chenille.

weight

The weight of the yarn refers to its heaviness and thickness. As a rule, you will use larger needles with heavier, thicker yarn. The heaviest yarn available is *super bulky,* used for thick, textured pieces. A bit lighter is *bulky,* which knits up quickly and warmly. *Worsted* yarn is one step down from bulky. Readily available and very popular, it's the yarn that most patterns call for. The lightest-weight yarns include *sport* and *fingering,* usually used for baby clothes, knitted lace, and finer clothing.

needles

It can be bewildering to walk into a yarn store for the first time and be faced with the many shapes and sizes of needles. Here are a few pointers.

needle materials

Metal or bamboo, wood or plastic? I recommend bamboo or wooden needles for beginners, as they aren't as slippery as metal and are warmer to the touch than plastic or metal. You may also find needles made of casein (a natural dairy product), designed to feel like antique tortoiseshell needles.

needle shapes

Single-point or *straight needles* are the traditional needles, with a knob on one end, usually used when creating flat pieces or sweater parts. They come in 10-, 12-, or 14-inch lengths. Select the needle length by the size of your project and the materials list given in the pattern.

Double-pointed needles are used for knitting smaller, tubular shapes such as socks and mittens, and for finishing off larger projects knit on circular needles. Double-pointed needles come in sets of 4 or 5 needles to a package.

Circular needles are basically two double-pointed needles joined by a plastic cord and are used for knitting larger projects in the round. Circular needles can be anywhere from 12 to 40 inches in length, allowing you to make seamless hats and bulky sweater bodies. You can also use them to knit flat pieces.

needle size

Needles come in sizes ranging from 0 (for very delicate doll clothes and collars) to size 19 (for extra-bulky scarves and sweaters that knit up in a flash). Most yarn packages specify which size works best for that type of yarn. Knitting patterns will also recommend appropriate needle sizes. If you're not sure of the size you need, ask someone who works at the store.

miscellaneous paraphernalia

A few additional items will help make your knitting projects go more smoothly. They're inexpensive and will prove useful time and time again.

crochet hook

At some point you will drop a stitch and not realize it until you've knit a few rows (or maybe more). You can carefully undo your work until you reach the problem spot and reknit, or you can find the top loop of the dropped stitch and reweave it into the fabric with the help of a crochet hook (see page 26).

gauge aid

This flat metal tool has holes that tell you the size of a needle so you can quickly find the appropriate ones. It also has a thick, open 90-degree angle with a ruler on each side. Place this directly on your knit swatch to quickly determine the number of stitches per inch.

point protectors

These small rubber caps fit on the tips of your needles to keep your work from slipping off when you put your project down. They fit size 3 to 15 needles.

row counter

This is useful when you're first learning to knit. I used mine a lot as a beginner because I was so focused on the basic mechanics of the craft that I often forgot how far along I was and found myself constantly having to painstakingly count rows.

scissors

A plain pair of sharp scissors is of utter necessity when working with yarn.

stitch holders

These resemble large safety pins and are used to hold stitches that you've set aside. For example, when making mittens or sweaters, you will have to set aside the thumbhole stitches and the armhole stitches, respectively, and come back to them later. Some knitters use safety pins, but they tend to snag on the yarn.

stitch markers

Place one of these small plastic rings in front of the first stitch when knitting in the round, and you'll never have to guess at your starting point. You can also make your own stitch marker with a simple knotted loop of yarn in a contrasting color.

tape measure

This comes in handy for measuring the length of scarves and for patterns in which you are directed to knit a certain number of inches rather than a certain number of rows.

yarn needles

These are a must for finishing any knit project. A yarn needle is a big, blunt sewing needle with a large eye used to weave loose ends into the body of your project.

yarn weight: conversion chart

Throughout this book you might notice that yarn weights will be listed in either ounces or grams. While there are no fast and steady rules as to why different yarn manufacturers use different units of measurements for their products, often times light-weight yarns such as mohair tend to be sold in grams as it allows the manufacturer to be more precise. We took our cues from the labels of the yarn used, and listed them accordingly. It's entirely possible that while shopping for your yarn you might find that the manufacturer has listed its weight in a different unit of measurement than the one specified in this book. For this purpose, we've included a conversion chart below.

One important thing to keep in mind is that yarn can be longer or shorter depending on how heavy or dense it is. For instance, a 4 ounce skein of bulky yarn might be 125 yards long while those same 4 ounces of worsted weight yarn might measure out to 190 yards.

It's usually a good idea to pay attention to both the weight and the length of your yarn when estimating how many skeins you will need to finish a project.

ounces	grams
1.76 ounces	50 grams
3.52 ounces	100 grams
2 ounces	56.69 grams
4 ounces	133.39 grams

how to knit

This chapter includes instructions for all the techniques you'll need to know to complete the projects in this book. You'll learn how to cast on and bind off, knit and purl, increase, decrease, and yarn over. It explains the difference between knitting on two needles and knitting in the round. It also offers advice for troubleshooting and where to go for help if you get stuck.

holding the needles

The first step in learning to knit is deciding how to hold the needles. There are a few variations; experiment until you find the way that feels most comfortable. The directions below are for both left- and right-handed knitters.

left hand

The needle holding the stitches rests in your left hand. The stitch nearest the end should be about 1 inch from the needle's tip. Hold the needle with your index finger at the first stitch. Or, if you're knitting Continenetal style, hold the needle with your middle finger at the first stitch (see page 19). Your thumb rests on the opposite side of the needle to stabilize it. The remaining three fingers curl under to balance the needle.

right hand

Rest your index finger on the top of the needle, about 2 inches from the tip. Place your thumb about an inch lower, on the opposite side. Lightly curl the remaining three fingers lower around the needle.

figure 1a, how to hold the needles
and yarn, positioning the yarn
American style

figure 1b

positioning the yarn

The two most common methods of knitting are American and Continental. In the American style, you hold and move the yarn with your right hand. In the Continental style, you hold and move the yarn with your left hand. Try both to see which you feel more comfortable with. Eventually you will want to know both styles, as it's helpful for Fair Isle knitting, in which you work with two colors of yarn at a time.

american style

The ball of yarn should be to your right. Rest the strand that leads from your left needle to the ball on top of your *right* index finger, then wrap it under your middle finger, over your third finger, and let the rest trail down to your ball under the little finger (figure 1a).

continental style

Place the ball of yarn to your left and weave the yarn that leads from your left needle to the ball over your *left* index finger, under the middle finger, over the third finger, and let it trail down to the ball under the little finger (figure 1b). If you are left-handed, you may find this method easier.

There are many other ways to hold the yarn. It needs to be neither too loose nor too tight as you work with it. Some people like to wrap the yarn loosely around a finger to help maintain the correct tension. Experiment and do what works best for you.

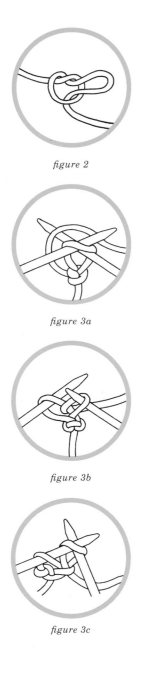

figure 2

figure 3a

figure 3b

figure 3c

casting on

All knitting begins with a **cast-on row.** The number of cast-on stitches determines the size of the piece you are knitting. There are several ways to cast on. The instructions here offer the method known as **knit cast-on,** which uses two needles. Practice with a pair of size 8 or 9 single-point, 10-inch needles and some acrylic yarn. Place the ball of yarn to your right and pull out a few feet of yarn.

1. Form a slipknot 8 inches from the end of the yarn. To do this, make a small loop of yarn. Pinch a second loop of yarn from the yarn end, about an inch below the first loop, pull it around and thread it through the backside of the first loop. Grasp the second loop and draw the first loop closed by pulling the yarn end that leads to the ball (figure 2). Slide the slipknot onto a needle and tighten the knot until it is a little larger in circumference than the needle. Hold the needle with the stitch in your left hand.

2. Taking the second needle in your right hand, thread the yarn that leads to the ball over your right index finger, below your middle finger, and over your third finger, letting the rest fall beneath your little finger down toward the ball (see figure 1a, page 19).

3. Insert your right needle through the front of the stitch on your left needle, forming an X with your needles (figure 3a). Raise your right index finger and loop yarn from the ball end around the right needle from back to front (figure 3b). Dip and pull the right needle toward you, away from the left needle, catching the newly formed loop (figure 3b).

4. Slip the new loop on the right needle onto your left needle (figure 3c). You now have two cast-on stitches on the left needle. Repeat until you have 20 or so stitches. You may want to practice casting on a few times before moving on to learning the knit stitch.

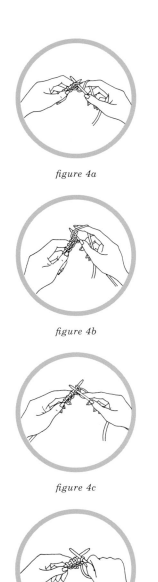

figure 4a

figure 4b

figure 4c

figure 4d

the knit stitch, american style

Make sure that your cast-on row is not twisted and that the bottoms (the chunky part) of the stitches are aligned and evenly spaced. Hold the needle with the cast-on row in your left hand. Hold the yarn American style, as directed in "Positioning the Yarn" (page 19), letting the rest fall beneath your little finger down toward the ball.

1. Insert your right needle through the first stitch on the left needle forming an X with your needle (figure 4a).

2. Raise your right index finger and loop the yarn around the right needle from back to front (figure 4b).

3. Dip and pull the right needle toward you, away from the left needle, catching the newly formed loop (figure 4c).

4. Leaving the new loop on your right needle, pull the right needle with the new stitch toward you, away from the left needle, and let the rest of the original stitch slip off the left needle. This is your first knit stitch (figure 4d).

5. Repeat until you reach the end of the row. At that point, you will shift the right-hand needle (which is now full of stitches) back to your left hand.

the knit stitch, continental style

Make sure that your cast-on row is not twisted and that the bottoms (the chunky part) of the stitches are aligned and evenly spaced. Hold the needle with the cast-on row in your left hand. Hold the yarn Continental style, as directed in "Positioning the Yarn" (page 19), letting the rest fall beneath your little finger down toward the ball.

1. Insert your right needle through the first stitch on the left needle, forming an X with your needles.

2. Raise your left index finger and loop the yarn around the right needle, wrapping it from left to right. Dip and pull the right needle toward you, away from the left needle, catching the newly formed loop.

3. Leaving the new loop on your right needle, pull the right needle with the new stitch toward you, away from the left needle, and let the rest of the original stitch slip off the left needle. This is your first knit stitch.

4. Repeat until you reach the end of the row. At that point, you will shift the right-hand needle (which is now full of stitches) back to your left hand.

You may find it helpful to remember the steps of the knit stitch with a traditional poem that has been handed down for generations:

In through the front door,
Once around the back,
Peek through the window,
And off jumps Jack.

Practice the knit stitch until you feel comfortable, and then move on to the purl stitch. You can do all of the patterns in the "First Projects" chapter using the knit stitch, casting on, and binding off. I suggest doing at least one of these projects now.

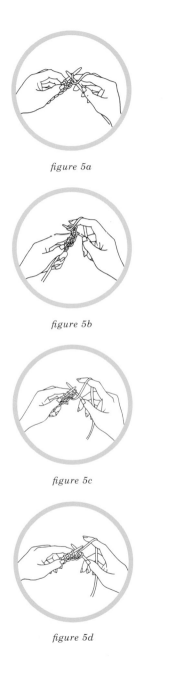

figure 5a

figure 5b

figure 5c

figure 5d

the purl stitch

When you made the knit stitch, you worked with the yarn held behind the left needle. When you make the purl stitch, you will be working with the yarn held **in front** of the left needle. Knit and purl are the two basic stitches that make up almost every other type of stitch in knitting, so once you learn them both you will be well on your way to becoming a master. Hold the needles and the yarn the same way you did for the knit stitch, either American or Continental style. The only difference is that you hold the yarn that leads to the ball **in front** of the left needle. If you hold it behind the needle, it will be impossible to catch it in the right way to form a purl stitch.

1. Insert your right needle through the first stitch on the left needle (figure 5a).

2. Raise your right index finger (or your left index finger, if you are knitting in the Continental style), and loop the yarn from the ball end around the right needle from back to front (figure 5b).

3. Dip and pull the right needle away from you, catching the newly formed loop (figure 5c).

4. Leaving the new loop on your right needle, pull the right needle with the new stitch away from you, and away from the left needle. Let the rest of the original stitch slip off the left needle. This is your first purl stitch (figure 5d).

5. Repeat until you reach the end of the row. At that point, you will shift the right-hand needle (which is now full of stitches) back to your left hand.

o o o

a note to beginners

Knitting and purling may seem a little awkward at first. Don't worry about your stitches looking uneven or messy. This is part of the learning process. You will also tend to knit tightly in the beginning to avoid dropping stitches and making mistakes. As you continue practicing, you will feel more and more comfortable with the needles, and your stitches will smooth out and loosen up.

As you knit, remember not to let your fingers sneak up too close to the tip of the needle or too far back toward the end, as this makes the stitches harder to work. You may also find yourself clutching at the needles, which eventually causes your hands to cramp. If you find yourself falling into these patterns, just take a deep breath, relax, and correct the situation. Before you know it, you will be knitting automatically and with ease.

o o o

knitting abbreviations

If you've compared this book to other knitting books, you may have noticed that **Knitting Pretty** doesn't use abbreviations in the patterns. Everything is written out in plain English. However, there is a whole language of knitting shorthand, which allows patterns to be written very economically but can be extremely unnerving to beginners.

Here is an example from a vintage Jack Frost baby blanket pattern: CO 162 sts. K 28 rows, then work in pattern as follows: Row 1—K 21, P 4, K 4, P 4, * K 6, P 4, K 4, P 4; repeat from * 5 times, ending K 21.

Eventually, you will want to know what these abbreviations mean, and when you're ready there is a table explaining them on page 116. But for now, just experience the joy of knitting without puzzling over complex and often confusing abbreviations.

o o o

figure 6a

figure 6b

figure 6c

binding off

So you've knit a good, long strip and you want to get it off the needles and secure it so it doesn't unravel. This process is called binding off.

1. Start at the beginning of a row and knit 2 stitches in the usual way. You now have 2 stitches on your right needle.

2. Insert your left needle into the front of the first stitch on your right needle (figure 6a).

3. Pull the first stitch over the top of the second stitch and off the needle (figures 6b and 6c). You now have 1 stitch on your right needle.

4. Knit one more stitch. Again, you have 2 stitches on your right needle. Repeat steps 2 and 3. Continue in this manner until 1 stitch remains on your right needle and none remain on your left. At this point cut the yarn (leaving about a 6-inch tail to weave in later) and draw the end of the yarn through the center of the final stitch. Pull to tighten it into a knot.

You can also bind off on a purl row. All you have to do is repeat the sequence above with purl stitches instead of knit stitches.

weaving in loose ends

You will be faced with many loose ends of yarn over the course of your knitting career—when you cast on, bind off, sew pieces together, or add a new color or an extra ball of yarn. All you need to do to hide these ends is to thread them, one by one, onto a yarn needle and weave the yarn into the edges or the wrong side of your knitting. When you feel the yarn end is secure (usually after about 3 inches), remove the needle and trim the yarn.

picking up dropped stitches

Even if you are very careful, you will eventually drop a stitch. While it's annoying, it's no reason to throw in the towel. Simply fix it with your trusty crochet hook. The dropped stitch will unravel downward into the fabric you've already knit, creating a ladder (figure 7). Here's what to do.

figure 7

1. Push the remaining stitches toward the knob end of your needle so they won't fall off. If you were working on a purl row (if the wrong side of the piece is facing you), turn the work around so the knit stitches are facing you.

2. Catch the top of the dropped loop with your crochet hook.

3. Slide the loop down below the hook, and use the hook itself to latch onto the rung of the ladder directly above the dropped stitch. Pull the rung through the loop, being careful not to twist it.

4. Use the hook to catch the next strand of the ladder. Keep going until you reach the needle, placing the last loop back where it belongs, on either your right or left knitting needle.

joining a new strand of yarn

When your yarn ball runs out before your piece is finished, you'll need to join a new strand of yarn. There are many ways to do this. I prefer to tie the new piece in (method 1), but everyone has a favorite method. Here are a few to choose from.

1. Join a new strand by tying the new strand around the old in a slipknot. This should be done at the beginning of a row. Slide the knot up as close as possible to the knit fabric, and just start knitting with the new ball. Later you will weave the loose ends into the knit piece.

2. If you are joining the same color of yarn, you can simply knit with both the new yarn and the old one for 2 or 3 stitches to secure it, and then continue on with new yarn alone. Again, you will go back later and weave the loose ends into the knit fabric. You may be afraid that the double-strand part will be lumpy, but it blends in nicely with the rest of the fabric.

3. If you must join yarn in the middle of a row, you may want to meld the new and old yarns together. Thread a yarn needle with the new yarn and weave it into the end of the old yarn for about 3 inches. Remove the needle and give the yarn a little pull to secure it and straighten it out. Leave the short tail on the wrong side of the knit piece, and trim it off later.

4. Occasionally, as when you start the thumb of a mitten or work around a baby bootie, you will have to join new yarn to nothing but a row of stitches. In this case, anchor the loose end of the new ball with your hand to prevent the yarn from slipping. It may feel akward, but after the first few stitches it will secure.

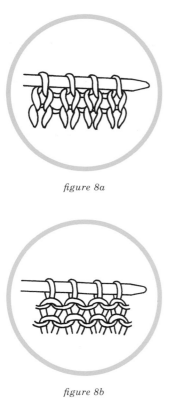

figure 8a

figure 8b

creating patterns with stitches

You've learned the two basic stitches you will use over and over again—the knit stitch and the purl stitch. But there are many ways to combine these stitches to create very different patterns and textures. Here are just a few.

garter stitch

This basic stitch is created simply by knitting every row. The knitted fabric looks the same on both sides with a series of ridges and does not curl at the edges. This is the easiest stitch.

stockinette stitch

In the stockinette stitch, you knit one row and purl the next. Most store-bought sweaters are knit predominantly in stockinette stitch. The knitted fabric has a smooth side that looks like it is formed of tiny V's and a bumpier side. The smooth side is usually used as the "right" or outer side of the garment. This stitch is rarely used in the borders of projects or in things like scarves because it curls at the edges.

Many patterns refer to the knit side of stockinette as the "right" side and to the purl side as the "wrong" side. If you have come back to a work in progress and can't remember which stitch to use next, just examine the stitches facing you as you hold the full needle in your left hand. If the stitches are smooth and flat (figure 8a), it's the right side and you should knit. If the stitches are bumpy (figure 8b), it's the wrong side and you should purl.

rib stitch

Ribbing is created when the knit and purl stitches alternate in a row. Ribbing is often seen on items that require snug, non-curling edges, such as sweaters and mittens. To make a knit 1, purl 1 ribbing, cast on an even number of stitches. Work across the row, knitting 1 stitch and purling the next. You'll need to move the yarn from back to front and vice versa in order to alternate stitches. When you reach the end of the row, repeat the same pattern of stitches for the next row. To make a knit 2, purl 2 ribbing, cast on an even number of stitches in a multiple of 4, as the pattern will repeat every 4 stitches. Work across the row, knitting 2 stitches and then purling 2 stitches. Repeat the same pattern for the next row.

seed stitch

This textured stitch, also called a moss stitch, is created by alternating knit and purl stitches from row to row. Cast on an even number of stitches and alternate between the knit and purl stitches as follows:

Row 1: Knit, purl, knit, purl, knit, purl, knit, purl, knit, purl . . .

Row 2: Purl, knit, purl, knit, purl, knit, purl, knit, purl, knit . . .

In other words, after the first row you purl the smooth stitches and knit the bumpy ones.

figure 9

increasing

Sometimes you'll need to make a piece of knitting wider, such as when you shape the sleeve of a sweater. The easiest way to increase is to turn one stitch into two by knitting or purling it twice.

1. Slide your needle into a stitch as if to knit, and wrap the yarn around the needle as usual. Catch the newly formed loop and pull it away with the right needle. Instead of letting the rest of the original stitch slide off the needle, leave the new loop on the right needle and the rest of the original stitch on the left.

2. Slip the right needle into the back of the original stitch and wrap the yarn around the needle again; then let it slide off onto the right needle (figure 9). You now have 2 stitches instead of 1.

figure 10a

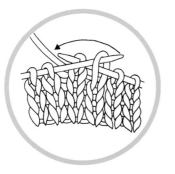

figure 10b

decreasing

Sometimes you will need to make a piece of knitting smaller or narrower, such as when you shape the top of a hat. Here are two basic techniques.

1. The easiest way to decrease is to knit or purl 2 stitches together. To do this, simply insert your right needle into two stitches on your left needle and knit or purl them as one, thus creating a single stitch where 2 stitches were previously. This kind of decrease slants to the right.

2. Another way of decreasing is with a technique known as *pass slipped stitch over*. This method is similar to the one described earlier for binding off. This type of decrease will slant to the left. Insert your needle into a stitch as if you were about to knit it. But don't knit it—instead, just slip it off onto the right needle (figure 10a). Knit the next stitch, and then slide the left needle into the front of the slipped stitch on the right needle. Pull the slipped stitch over the stitch in front of it and let it fall off the needle (figure 10b). You now have 1 stitch where you previously had 2.

yarn over

The **yarn over** technique creates the open, lacy look often seen in shawls. This technique increases the number of stitches on your needle and can be done on the knit or purl side.

To do a yarn over on the knit side, wrap the yarn over and around the right needle, from front to back (figure 11a), and then knit the next stitch (or knit 2 stitches together if directed to do so). When you work across the next row, you will see that an open space has been formed.

To do a yarn over on the purl side, bring the yarn from the front of the right needle over the top and around the back (figure 11b), and then purl the next stitch.

figure 11a

fringe

Adding fringe to scarves or shawls adds extra flair, and it's easy to do. First, cut a length of yarn that's double your desired length of fringe. Fold the yarn in half and push the looped end of the yarn through one stitch on the edge of the knit item where you want fringe to be. (You can use your yarn needle or a crochet hook to help with this.) Draw the cut ends of the yarn through the loop, and then tighten to make a knot. Trim the ends to even them up.

figure 11b

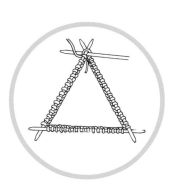

figure 12, knitting in the round,
4 double-pointed needles

knitting in the round

You can make anything—sweaters, hats, mittens—by knitting it in pieces and then sewing it together. But knitting in the round has several advantages that flat knitting doesn't. First, you are creating a stronger, seamless piece. Second, you work faster on circular needles because you knit in a continuous circle rather than flipping the piece over constantly to work a front and a back.

When you knit in the round, you create a circle of stitches and work in "rounds" rather than rows. There are two ways to knit in the round. Use a set of four double-pointed needles for smaller projects with tighter rounds, to handle the small number of stitches per needle (figure 12). When you are casting on with double-pointed needles, it's easiest to cast all of the stitches required onto one needle and then divide them among the three needles, rather than trying to cast 8 onto one needle, 10 onto another, and 8 more onto a third. Circular needles are great for larger pieces like sweaters and hats, both of which have enough stitches to stretch around a longer cord.

To join a row of stitches into a circle, make sure that your work is not twisted, place a stitch marker in front of the first stitch on your right needles, and join the first stitch to the last simply by knitting them together. This may seem a little awkward in the beginning, so rest the needles in your lap while you do it. Continue to work in a circle until the desired number of rounds is obtained. Your stitch marker indicates the beginning of the round. One of the beauties of knitting in the round is that you can create the stockinette stitch using only the knit stitch: Since you are working in a circle, you never have to turn your work and purl.

making seams

Sewing together pieces of knitting is trickier than sewing pieces of cloth because you're working with a bulkier fabric, and you have to remember to line up stitches and rows. It's always best to pin the pieces together before sewing; otherwise, you will spend a lot of time making sure the ends match up. In addition, you should never make seams too tight.

Knitting is elastic, and your seams should be as well. I recommend starting out with a small project like the Petite Pillow Cover (page 92). Experiment with different techniques, and don't hesitate to pull out a few stitches or even an entire seam in order to sew something you're completely satisfied with.

A few of the many different ways to make seams are described below. Whatever method you use, you should always use a yarn needle threaded with about 18 inches of the same type of yarn you used to make your knit fabric. When you make your stitches, be careful not to split the yarn. Instead, pass your needle through the spaces in the stitches.

figure 13a

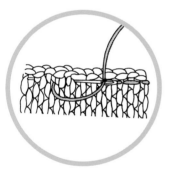

figure 13b

backstitch

The backstitch is commonly used to join shoulder, sleeve, and side seams. With this method you will be creating a thin inner seam, so you want to stay close to the edge of the fabric while sewing. (Don't go deeper than 2 stitches in.)

1. Match the pieces you are sewing together, with wrong sides out. Make sure that your stitches are lined up, and pin the pieces in place.

2. Thread your yarn needle with the same yarn you used to knit the item. Take a stitch through both pieces of fabric, coming up $\frac{1}{2}$ inch away from the corner. Leave about a 6-inch tail of yarn to weave in later.

3. Take a short stitch back to the corner (figure 13a). Secure the yarn by repeating this stitch.

4. Insert the needle again $\frac{1}{2}$ inch in front of the stitch you just made, coming up from the back through to the front of the fabric (figure 13b).

5. Insert the needle in front of the first stitch and sew through to the back, filling in the gap between the stitches.

6. Continue in this manner until you reach the end. Keep the stitches even, and make sure you're not pulling the yarn too tight.

Vary the length of the stitch depending on the fineness of the fabric you are seaming. For instance, you may want to make stitches $\frac{1}{4}$ inch long when sewing seams in baby clothes and $\frac{3}{4}$ inch long for seams in bulky sweaters. If seams made with bulky yarn seem too chunky, use the overcast stitch, described next, to join the pieces instead.

overcast and mattress stitches

The overcast and mattress stitches both make flatter seams than the backstitch. They are great for sewing pillow seams, joining borders or edgings, and joining sections of ribbing. You can also use them to make flatter seams in sweaters.

overcast stitch

1. Match the pieces you are sewing together, with wrong sides out and the stitches lined up. You will be working close to the edge of the fabric, no deeper than the first stitch on each side.

2. Thread your yarn needle with the same yarn you used to knit the item. Starting at the corner, take a stitch through both pieces of fabric, leaving about a 6-inch tail to weave in later. Secure the yarn by inserting the needle back into the same hole, from back to front.

3. Sew through the next matching ridge of fabric, again bringing the thread through from back to front. The yarn will wrap around the edge of the fabric.

4. Continue in this manner until you reach the end of the seam (figure 14). Keep the stitches even, and make sure you're not pulling the yarn too tight.

figure 14

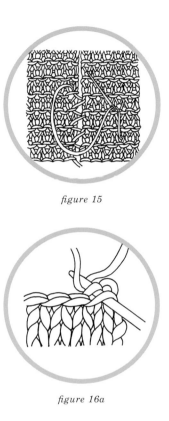

figure 15

figure 16a

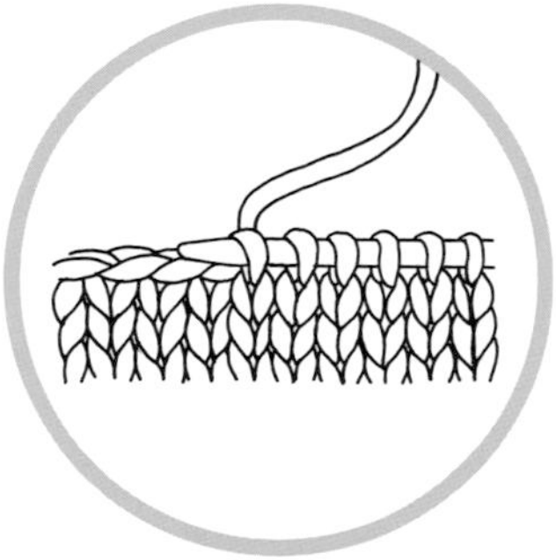

figure 16b

mattress stitch

1. Match the pieces edge to edge, with the stitches lined up and both right sides facing you.

2. Thread your yarn needle with the same yarn you used to knit the item. Starting at the left corner and leaving about a 6-inch tail to weave in later, pull the yarn through the middle of the first stitch on the right side.

3. Sew diagonally to the left, coming up in the center of the first stitch in the row above.

4. Repeat, weaving from left to right to left to right, until you reach the end of the section to be joined (figure 15).

picking up stitches

Sometimes you will need to pick up stitches from an otherwise finished edge in order to create the collar of a sweater, form the thumb of a mitten, or knit the outer edge of a baby bootie.

To do this, hold the knit item before you so that the outside of the garment is facing you. The edge where the stitches are to be picked up should be at the top. Your pattern will specify how many stitches to pick up, and you will need to space them evenly. To pick up a stitch, insert your knitting needle into the edge of the piece, from front to back, and pull a loop of new yarn through to the front (figure 16a). Continue until you've picked up the number of stitches you need, spacing them evenly across (figure 16b). If the picked-up stitches seem skewed or have a big gap somewhere, take them out and try again.

gauge

Gauge refers to the number of stitches per inch and rows per inch. It will change radically depending on the type of yarn you use, the stitch pattern you are knitting, the size of your needles, and how tightly or loosely you tend to knit. (This can vary, depending on your mood!) Many patterns specify a gauge to help the knitter more closely achieve the desired results. With that said, gauge is not the be-all and end-all of successful knitting, and for some projects it isn't even an issue. Most of the projects in these pages don't require you to pay much attention to gauge; in a few, however, the gauge is critical. On larger projects, such as sweaters, more or fewer stitches per inch means the difference between small and large in the finished project.

To determine gauge, you need to knit a small sample, or swatch, of fabric. You must use the specific yarn and needles that you'll be using for the project, and the swatch should be knit in the stitch you will be using. A simple recipe for a 5-inch swatch follows.

1. Check the pattern to see how many stitches per inch it calls for. For example, the gauge may be 4 stitches per inch on size 8 needles. Use size 8 needles to cast on at least 20 stitches. Knit in the stitch specified in the project directions until the swatch is at least 5 inches long.

2. Bind off and flatten the swatch out beneath your gauge aid, making sure that your stitches are lined up straight both horizontally and vertically and that the stitches at the left and bottom of your swatch window are not partially covered by the gauge aid.

3. Count the number of stitches across. If you knit 4 stitches per inch with this yarn, you can follow the pattern exactly. If you knit more or fewer, you should adjust the number of stitches you cast on or change the needle size. It's

always easier to adjust your needle size rather than the number of stitches on complicated projects such as sweaters, as one adjustment in the number of stitches leads to many other adjustments.

If you don't have a gauge aid, you can use a steam iron to steam the swatch a bit so it flattens out. (Don't touch the iron to the wool.) Then pin the swatch flat and use a ruler to measure the stitches per inch and rows per inch.

blocking

Blocking is a finishing technique that smoothes out stitches and coaxes knit pieces into the desired shape. To block your piece, first dampen it with water or steam, then gently shape it on a flat surface and allow it to dry. You do not need to block acrylic pieces, and you should never block ribbing, as it flattens out. Blocking is best for wool, and it gives a professional, finished look to sweaters. There are many different approaches to blocking. Here are a few.

1. Don't bother. If your pieces are knit smoothly and the stitches are even, you can just ignore this step.

2. After you have sewn together your sweater and spread the finished project out to look it over, use a steam iron to dampen it into smoothness. Be careful not to let the iron touch the wool. If it does, the wool will burn.

3. Place your knit items flat between two damp towels and let them dry naturally.

4. Dampen the knit item (it should not be wringing wet), shape it, and pin it to a blocking board, using nonrusting pins. Let it dry naturally.

   note: Never use blocking to try to stretch or shrink two knit pieces so that they match each other. It doesn't work. If you have accidentally made one side of a sweater too small, blocking is not the way to fix it. Your only option is to unravel the piece and knit it again.

where to get help

Inevitably there will be times when you are frustrated, annoyed, and irritated. Maybe you just noticed that you dropped a stitch about 10 rows back. Or perhaps your yarn is in a huge tangle and you have to stop to rewind it. Maybe you are at a particular point in a pattern and just can't figure out the next step, no matter how many times you reread it. You can probably handle dropped stitches and tangles on your own, but for other problems, don't be afraid to ask someone else for help.

Who should you ask? The best person would be a family member or friend who knits. But sometimes this isn't an option. In that case, try asking the staff at the store where you purchased your yarn; they will usually be happy to help. You can also visit the Knitting Guild of America's Web site (see "Resources," page 114) and post your question on the message boards you can link to from there. You are not alone. Lots of people out there knit, and knitters are almost always more than happy to share their knowledge.

first
projects

bookmark

Remember laminated bookmarks with yarn tassels—the ones that usually had some saying you thought was cute when you were eight but were mortified by later? Why not go one step further and make a bookmark entirely out of yarn? Whenever I teach people how to knit, I strongly suggest this as a first project. It's not only quick and easy, but the finished project makes an unusual and practical gift. Plus, it's a great way to practice the knit stitch and casting on and binding off.

1

difficulty level

techniques

Casting on, page 20

Garter stitch, page 28

Binding off, page 25

Weaving in loose ends, page 26

o o o

you will need

1 ball (100 grams) acrylic or wool worsted weight yarn

1 pair size 8 needles

Scissors

Yarn needle

directions

1. Cast on 18 stitches, leaving an 8-inch tail (this will be woven in to make the tassel later on).

2. Knit 8 rows of garter stitch.

3. Bind off, leaving an 8-inch tail.

4. Using your yarn needle, weave the tails into the center of the top edge of the bookmark and loop both pieces into a knot at the edge of the book-mark. This forms your tassel. Trim the ends to make them even.

5. If you'd like to add another color to the tassel to make it a little fancier, follow the directions on page 32 and add a piece of fringe.

improvisation idea: Knit 2 skinny strands of different-colored yarn simultaneously (hold them as one strand) for a slightly wilder effect.

plain old scarf

This is the second project I recommend for beginning knitters. It's like a gigantic bookmark. You cast on, knit for quite a while, and then bind off. By the time you're done, you'll be aching to move on to the purl stitch. Plus you'll have a warm and wonderful scarf to sport around town. I've included instructions for using two colors, as it's fun to watch the scarf grow stripe by stripe, but feel free to stick to one color on your first scarf. Cast on more stitches for a wider scarf, fewer for a narrower one.

1

difficulty level

techniques

Casting on, page 20

Garter stitch, page 28

Joining a new strand of yarn, page 27

Binding off, page 25

Weaving in loose ends, page 26

o o o

you will need

4 balls (50 grams each) of acrylic or wool worsted weight yarn, in 2 different colors

1 pair size 8 needles

Scissors

Yarn needle

Row counter (optional)

directions

1. Cast on 22 stitches.

2. Knit 44 rows of garter stitch.

3. Join yarn 2 to yarn 1, leaving about a 6-inch tail of each.

4. Knit 44 rows of garter stitch. Note: There is no law that says the stripes have to be the same width, so feel free to experiment as you wish. Just make certain to always switch yarns on the same side of the scarf, as the first row of knitting after each switch forms a 2-color pattern on one side.

5. Repeat steps 3 and 4 until you're satisfied with the length of the scarf.

6. Bind off.

7. Using your yarn needle, weave all loose ends into the edges of the scarf and trim them.

improvisation idea: For a more interesting texture, knit 2 different yarns at the same time, such as a bouclé and a worsted, holding them as one strand.

dishcloth

I used to be a sponge person. But when my aunt gave me one of these handy cotton cloths, I never looked back. Practical and economical, dishcloths knit up quickly and keep on going—you just wash them and use again. My aunt has used one particularly sturdy specimen for seven years! When you're ready for more of a challenge, try the Company Dishcloth (page 95).

1

difficulty level

techniques

Casting on, page 20

Garter stitch, page 28

Binding off, page 25

Weaving in loose ends, page 26

o o o

you will need

1   ball (2 ounces) 100% cotton
    worsted weight yarn

1   pair size 7 needles

Scissors

Yarn needle

Row counter (optional)

directions

1. Cast on 32 stitches.

2. Knit 72 rows of garter stitch.

3. Bind off.

4. Using your yarn needle, weave all loose ends into the edges of the cloth, and trim them.

5. Scrub away!

improvisation idea: Just because it's a dishcloth doesn't mean it has to be a boring color. Go wild!

chapter

4

old favorites

ice-skating scarf

This scarf is soft, long, warm, and a cinch to knit. What more can you ask for? Using only the knit stitch, alternate rows of worsted with bouclé to create a very fancy woven effect. And by leaving a 7-inch tail of yarn on each end of the scarf every time you switch yarns, you will create a dramatic fringe that swirls gracefully in your wake, both on and off the ice.

2

difficulty level

techniques

Casting on, page 20

Joining a new strand of yarn, page 27

Garter stitch, page 28

Binding off, page 25

o o o

you will need

2 balls (100 grams each) soft worsted weight yarn, such as llama or merino wool

1 ball (50 grams) bouclé yarn

1 size 11 circular needle, 29 inches or longer

Scissors

Ruler or tape measure

directions

1. Holding 2 strands of the worsted weight yarn as one, cast on 140 stitches, leaving at least a 7-inch tail at the beginning. Cut the yarn, leaving at least a 7-inch tail at the end (this will create your fringe).

2. Row 1: Attach the bouclé yarn at the base of the freshly cut worsted-weight strand, leaving a 7-inch tail. Knit to the end. Cut the yarn, leaving a 7-inch tail.

3. Row 2: Attach a double strand of worsted at the base of the freshly cut bouclé strand and knit the second row, leaving 7-inch tails at both ends.

4. Repeat steps 2 and 3 until you have 11 rows of worsted (remember, don't count the cast-on row) and 12 rows of bouclé.

5. Attach a double strand of worsted, leaving a 7-inch tail, and bind off *loosely*. If you bind off too tightly, the scarf will still be warm and lovely, but it will be slightly semicircular instead of straight. Check the tension after 30 stitches.

6. Using the ruler or tape measure, trim the fringe to 7 inches and try it on!

improvisation idea: Cast on 225 stitches for a scarf that will nearly sweep the floor. You will need to use extra yarn to maintain a nice thickness.

super-long ribbed scarf

Who doesn't love a nice, long ribbed scarf? Worked in knit 3, purl 3 ribbing using bulky yarn, this scarf has wide ribs and will stretch to about 6 feet. That may sound like a lot, but when you work with bulky yarn you need to make scarves longer to compensate for their thickness. Make sure to choose a nice soft yarn.

2

difficulty level

techniques

Casting on, page 20

Rib stitch, page 29

Joining a new strand of yarn, page 27

Binding off, page 25

Weaving in loose ends, page 26

o o o

you will need

3   skeins (4 ounces each) bulky acrylic or wool yarn

1   pair size 10½ needles

Scissors

Tape measure

Yarn needle

directions

1.   Cast on 33 stitches.

2.   Row 1: Work in knit 3, purl 3 ribbing to the end of the row. You will end with knit 3.

3.   Row 2: Work in purl 3, knit 3 ribbing to end of the row. You will end with purl 3.

4.   Repeat steps 2 and 3 until the scarf measures 6 feet.

5.   Bind off.

6.   Using your yarn needle, weave the loose ends into the scarf, and trim them.

improvisation idea: To create a more dramatic scarf, use 5 skeins of yarn (it will be 10 feet long!) and add fringe to the ends.

comfy ribbed hat

This isn't one of those tight, itchy $3 hats you can get on the street. Knit with soft bulky yarn, the Comfy Ribbed Hat (see hat on the left in the photograph on page 57) haloes your head in a thick woolen cloud and makes a great companion to the Super-Long Ribbed Scarf.

3

difficulty level

techniques

Casting on, page 20

Knitting in the round, page 33

Rib stitch, page 29

Decreasing, page 31

Weaving in loose ends, page 26

o o o

you will need

1   skein (4 ounces) bulky wool yarn

1   size 11 circular needle, 16 inches long

4   size 10 double-pointed needles

1   stitch marker

Tape measure

Scissors

Yarn needle

directions

1.   Cast 64 stitches onto the circular needle.

2.   Insert the stitch marker—this will mark the beginning of each new round.

3.   Join the stitches into a circle and work in knit 2, purl 2 ribbing until the hat measures 10 inches. You will now begin to decrease for the crown.

4.   For the next 2 rounds, decrease by always knitting 2 stitches together. When the stitches will not reach around the circular needle anymore, switch to double-pointed needles. To do this, knit off the circular needle onto 1 double-pointed needle at a time, dividing the stitches among 3 needles (you will be using the fourth needle to knit with). After the first round of decreasing, you will have 32 stitches on your needles; after the second you will have 16.

5.   Cut the yarn, leaving a 12-inch tail. Use your yarn needle to thread the tail through the remaining 16 stitches. Pull the yarn tight and knot to secure.

6.   Fold the bottom of the hat over to create a 2½-inch brim. Weave the loose ends of yarn into the hat, and trim them.

   improvisation idea: Knit the first 4 inches in a different color to make a fancier fold-up brim.

sculpted hat

This is the warmest hat you will ever wear. It's knit using two strands of yarn simultaneously, and the seed stitch pattern gives it an interesting but not too busy texture. I call it sculpted because it is so thick it can stand up by itself.

3

difficulty level

techniques

Casting on, page 20

Knitting in the round, page 33

Rib stitch, page 29

Seed stitch, page 29

Decreasing, page 31

Weaving in loose ends, page 26

o o o

you will need

2 skeins (4 ounces each) wool or acrylic worsted weight yarn

1 size 11 circular needle, 16 inches long

4 size 10 double-pointed needles

1 stitch marker

Scissors

Yarn needle

Row counter (optional)

directions

1. Holding 2 strands of worsted weight yarn as one, cast 50 stitches onto the circular needle.

2. Insert the stitch marker—this will mark the beginning of each new round.

3. Join the stitches into a circle and work 4 rounds in knit 1, purl 1 ribbing.

4. At the beginning of round 5, knit 2 stitches together. You now have 49 stitches on your needles. Purl the next stitch, knit the next, and so on. Continue for 25 more rounds in knit 1, purl 1 pattern. You are now creating the seed stitch pattern.

5. At the beginning of round 31, you will start to decrease to make the crown of the hat. For the next 2 rounds, decrease by always knitting 2 stitches together. Because you have an odd number of stitches, just knit the last stitch. When the stitches will not reach around the circular needle anymore, switch to double-pointed needles. To do this, knit off the circular needle onto 1 double-pointed needle at a time, dividing the stitches among 3 needles (you will be using the fourth needle to knit with).

6. After the first round of decreasing you will have 25 stitches on your needle; after the second you will have 13. Cut the yarn, leaving a 12-inch tail. Use your yarn needle to thread the tail through the remaining stitches. Pull the yarn tight, and weave in and trim the ends.

improvisation ideas: Make a taller, bigger hat by knitting 35 rows total before decreasing. You could also knit the first 4 rounds in a contrasting color.

roll-up hat

Like the Wiggly Worm Scarf on page 65, the Roll-Up Hat (pictured on the right, facing page) takes advantage of stockinette's natural curl to create a roll-up border at the bottom of the hat. And because it is worked on circular needles, you will use only the knit stitch to create it. This is a very popular hat, and almost every yarn company has a version of the pattern.

2

difficulty level

techniques

Casting on, page 20

Knitting in the round, page 33

Stockinette stitch, page 28

Decreasing, page 31

Weaving in loose ends, page 26

o o o

you will need

1   skein (4 ounces) wool or acrylic worsted weight yarn

1   size 7 circular needle, 16 inches long

4   size 7 double-pointed needles

1   stitch marker

Tape measure

Scissors

Yarn needle

directions

1.   Cast 76 stitches onto the circular needle.

2.   Insert the stitch marker—this will mark the beginning of each new round.

3.   Join the stitches into a circle, and work in stockinette stitch (knit only, since you're working in the round) until the hat measures 9 inches from the bottom of the unrolled base to the top of the knit fabric. You will now begin to decrease for the crown.

4.   For the next 2 rounds, decrease by always knitting 2 stitches together. When the stitches will not reach around the circular needle anymore, switch to double-pointed needles. To do this, knit off the circular needle onto 1 double-pointed needle at a time, dividing the stitches among 3 needles (you will be using the fourth needle to knit with). After the first round of decreasing, you will have 38 stitches on your needles; after the second you will have 19.

5.   Cut the yarn, leaving a 12-inch tail. Use your yarn needle to thread the tail through the remaining stitches. Pull the yarn tight, knot to secure, and weave in and trim the ends.

improvisation idea: To make a hat that's bigger and a little looser, cast on 80 stitches and knit until it measures 10 inches before the decrease.

warmest mittens

When it's late at night and the cold winds blow, you'll be glad you made these toasty mittens. Knit in the round with thick worsted wool, this project is a good one to try after mastering the Sculpted Hat. (In fact, the leftover yarn from the hat will make a whole pair of mittens.) This pattern fits an average woman's hand if you tend to knit tightly. For loose knitters or smaller hands, use size 3 and 4 double pointed needle instead. To create a larger mitten, move up a size or two with your needles.

4

difficulty level

techniques

Casting on, page 20

Knitting in the round, page 33

Rib stitch, page 29

Stockinette stitch, page 28

Increasing, page 30

Decreasing, page 31

Picking up stitches, page 37

Weaving in loose ends, page 26

→

directions

for the hand:

1. Cast 36 stitches on a size 4 double-pointed needle. Divide the stitches among 3 of the needles, 12 stitches per needle. You will be using the fourth needle to knit with.

2. Join the stitches into a circle and work 22 rounds in knit 2, purl 2 ribbing. This is the ribbed cuff.

3. Round 23: Work in stockinette stitch (knit only, since you're working in the round). Switch to the size 5 needles by substituting a 5 for a 4 as you knit around. Set the size 4 needles aside.

4. Knit 1 more round (for a total of 2 rounds on the number 5 needles). You will now begin to increase to match the shape of the hand and to create the thumb gusset.

5. Knit 1 stitch and place one of the stitch markers immediately after it. Increase 1 by knitting through the front and the back of the next stitch, then knit 1. Place the second marker. There are now 3 stitches between the markers. Increase 1, then knit to the end of the round.

→

you will need

1 skein (4 ounces) acrylic or wool worsted weight yarn

4 size 4 double-pointed needles

4 size 5 double-pointed needles

2 stitch markers

Stitch holder

Scissors

Yarn needle

Row counter (optional)

6. Knit 2 rounds, slipping the markers from your left to right needle as you go.

7. Knit 1, slip the marker to your right needle, increase 1, knit 1, increase 1. There are 5 stitches between the markers. Knit to the end of the round, and knit 2 more rounds.

8. Repeat step 7, increasing after the first marker and before the second one until you have 13 stitches between the markers. (Knit the additional 2 rounds after each increase round.)

9. Knit 1 stitch as if you were starting a new round, then take the first marker off and slide the 13 stitches off the needle and onto the stitch holder. You will use these stitches later to create the thumb. Take the second marker off. You will now be working 35 stitches on 3 needles.

10. Knit 25 rounds.

11. Begin decreasing for the mitten tip. For the next 4 rounds, knit 4 stitches and then knit 2 together, repeating throughout the round.

12. For the last 2 rounds, knit 3 stitches, and then knit 2 together, repeating throughout the round.

13. Cut a 12-inch tail and use your yarn needle to draw the tail through the remaining stitches. Pull the yarn tight, knot to secure, and weave in the ends.

for the thumb:

1. Slip the 13 reserved stitches from the stitch holder onto 2 size 5 needles, placing 7 stitches on one needle and 6 on the other.

2. Using a third size 5 needle, pick up 3 stitches in the space between the first 2 needles to form a triangle.

3. Starting on the right side of the third needle, knit a round, leaving an 8-inch tail to weave in later.

4. Knit 14 more rounds.

5. Begin decreasing to create the thumb tip. For 1 round, knit 1 stitch and then knit 2 together, repeating throughout.

6. For the final round, knit 2 together throughout.

7. Cut an 8-inch tail and use your yarn needle to draw the yarn through the remaining stitches. Pull it tight, knot to secure, and weave in and trim the ends. Gently tighten the tail at the base of the thumb and weave it in.

8. Repeat steps from casting on for the hand to make the second mitten!

improvisation idea: Choose 3 different colors and switch to another one every 10 rows.

slippers

Slippers are a good early project. They aren't technically difficult, and they knit up quickly. Because they are stretchy, the slippers from this pattern will fit up to a ladies' size 9½. If you want to knit a larger size, follow the directions in the parentheses.

2

difficulty level

techniques

Casting on, page 20

Garter stitch, page 28

Binding off, page 25

Rib stitch, page 29

Making seams, page 34

Weaving in loose ends, page 26

o o o

you will need

2   balls (4 ounces each) acrylic or wool bulky yarn (acrylic washes easily)

1   pair size 10 needles

Tape measure

Scissors

Yarn needle

directions

1. Cast on 36 (42) stitches.

2. Knit all rows in garter stitch until the piece measures 4½ (5) inches.

3. At the beginning of the next row, bind off 4 (7) stitches. You will have 32 (35) stitches on your needle. Repeat this on the next row. For both sizes, you will have 28 stitches on your needle.

4. Work in garter stitch for 2 more inches, until the piece measures 6½ (7) inches.

5. Now you will begin to shape the toe. Work the next 10 rows in knit 1, purl 1 ribbing.

6. Cut the yarn, leaving a 12-inch tail. Use your yarn needle to draw the tail through the remaining stitches. Pull the yarn tight and knot to secure. You will see the toe take shape as you do so.

7. Sew up the toe and the top of the slipper, using the overcast or mattress stitch. Weave in and trim the loose ends.

8. Sew up the back of the slipper. Weave in and trim the loose ends.

9. Repeat steps 1 through 8 to make the second slipper!

improvisation idea: To make a more elfin slipper with a fold-over top, cast on 50 stitches in step 1, and bind off 11 stitches on each side instead of 4 in step 3.

adorable knits

for kids of all ages

wiggly worm scarf

Worms are not only good for the environment, they can also help keep you warm. I first made this for a three-year-old, but I have since found that lots of thirty-year-olds like them too. Take advantage of stockinette's natural tendency to curl to knit a silly and sassy scarf.

3

difficulty level

techniques

Casting on, page 20

Stockinette stitch, page 28

Increasing, page 30

Decreasing, page 31

Weaving in loose ends, page 26

→

directions

1. Cast on 3 stitches. (You are beginning at the tail.)

2. You will be working the entire worm in stockinette stitch and increasing as you go, so follow these directions to make the thin part of the tail:
   Row 1: Knit.
   Row 2: Purl.
   Row 3: Knit.
   Row 4: Purl.
   Row 5: Knit 1, increase 1 by knitting through the front and back of the stitch, then knit to end of row.
   Row 6: Purl.
   Row 7: Knit.
   Row 8: Purl.
   Row 9: Knit until 1 stitch remains, then increase 1 by knitting through the front and back of the last stitch.
   Row 10: Purl.
   Row 11: Knit.
   Row 12: Purl.
   Row 13: Knit.
   Row 14: Purl.

   →

you will need

1   ball (100 grams) acrylic or wool worsted weight yarn (green to make an inchworm or red for a red worm)

1   pair size 9 needles

Tape measure

Scissors

Yarn needle

2   buttons for the worm's eyes

Sewing needle and thread

3.   You will begin to work in a 10-row pattern that will widen the worm's body. You will increase by 2 stitches (one at the beginning and one at the end of a row) every 10 rows.
Row 15: Knit 1, increase 1, knit to last stitch, increase 1 by knitting through the front and back of the last stitch. Knit the next 9 rows in stockinette stitch.

4.   Repeat step 3 until you have 25 stitches on your needle.

5.   Continue working in stockinette stitch until the scarf measures 48 inches.

6.   You will now begin to decrease for the head. Knit 1, knit 2 together. Repeat this pattern across the row, and knit the final, single stitch.

7.   Purl the next row.

8.   Knit 2 together across the row, and knit the final, single stitch.

9.   Cut the yarn, leaving an 8-inch tail, and draw it through the remaining stitches and knot to secure. Use your yarn needle to weave in loose ends.

10.   Sew eye buttons in appropriate places at the head of the scarf. Please make sure buttons are sewn on securely, as they may pose a choking hazard.

improvisation ideas: Knit with variegated yarn to create a striped worm. Or cut a forked tongue out of felt, sew it onto the head, and turn your worm into a snake!

sock puppet couture

This is a great way to use up scrap yarn and to make people happy. The great thing about these knit outfits is that you don't have to sew them onto the puppet's body. They expand with your hand!

techniques

Casting on, page 20

Garter stitch, page 28

Binding off, page 25

Weaving in loose ends, page 26

Knitting in the round, page 33

Rib stitch, page 29

o o o

you will need

Scraps of worsted weight yarn (1 ounce)

4 size 6 double-pointed needles

Tape measure

Scissors

Yarn needle

Felt scraps, buttons, or googly eyes

directions

for the scarf:

1. Cast 5 stitches onto a size 6 double-pointed needle.

2. Knit all rows in garter stitch until the scarf measures 16 inches.

3. Bind off. Cut the yarn, and use the yarn needle to weave in the loose ends.

for the tube top:

1. Cast 28 stitches onto a size 6 double-pointed needle. Divide the stitches among 3 needles, with 8, 8, and 12 stitches on the needles.

2. Join the stitches into a circle, and work in knit 3, purl 1 ribbing until the top measures 5 inches.

3. Bind off. Cut the yarn and use the yarn needle to weave in the loose ends.

note: These puppets have eyes cut out of felt scraps, sewn on with black thread. Other eye options include buttons and glue-on googly eyes. The hair is braided yarn anchored to a center knot and bouclé gathered with a loop of thread and then sewn to the sock. Lips were made using embroidery floss. The sweater is a beer cozy with skinny beer cozies attached for arms. The hat consists of 20 cast-on stitches, 3 rounds of ribbing, then periodic decreases to make it taper to a point.

improvisation idea: Instead of giving your best friend a hat and mitten set for his or her birthday, give a matching hat and sock puppet set.

sky blue baby blanket

My friend Anita made this simple project for a niece who wanted a comforting small blanket to watch videos with. Shades of blue, purple, and gold—what could be prettier than the colors of the sky? You determine the size of your squares by the number of stitches you cast on. Big patches of color or tiny ones—it's up to you! I used worsted wool and number 9 needles on the sample, and I cast on 22 stitches to make 6½-by-6½-inch squares. Yours may vary a little in size depending on the type of wool and how tightly you knit. Don't worry; as long as all of the squares are about the same size they'll fit together well.

2

difficulty level

techniques

Casting on, page 20

Garter stitch, page 28

Binding off, page 25

Overcast stitch, page 36

Weaving in loose ends, page 26

directions for each square

1. Cast on 22 stitches.

2. You will be working each square in garter stitch, knitting every row. Knit until you have a square that is as high as it is wide. You can determine this by measuring with your tape measure or by folding the square in half diagonally to create two equal triangles.

3. Bind off.

4. Repeat steps 1 through 3 until you have completed 24 squares.

5. Lay the squares out on the floor and arrange them in an appealing manner, 4 across and 6 high. The blanket will be more visually interesting if you alternate the direction of the squares between horizontal and vertical. Take another look. When you are satisfied with the arrangement, you are ready to start putting the blanket together.

6. Sew the squares into rows, and then sew the rows together, using the overcast stitch.

you will need

6 balls (100 grams each) acrylic or wool worsted weight yarn in a variety of colors (5 for the squares and 1 to sew them together)

1 pair size 9 needles

Tape measure

Scissors

Yarn needle

Row counter (optional)

7. After you have assembled the blanket, you will be left with a lot of loose yarn ends on the back. Tie the ends where 4 squares meet into strong (but not too tight) knots, and then trim them to an inch. This is similar to the technique used in tying quilts. For the yarn on the edges, use your yarn needle to weave the loose tails of yarn into the inside of the seam until secure, then trim them.

improvisation ideas: Use earth tones or fall colors for similarly comforting blankets. Or be more whimsical and make a hot dog–colored blanket (mustard or relish—it's up to you).

cute-as-can-be baby booties

I always know someone who is having a baby. What better gift to help welcome the little tyke into the world than a pair of traditional baby booties? They knit up in no time, will keep baby's feet warm, and will thrill the proud parents. Because booties incorporate many different operations in a small space, they can be tricky, so it's important to know where you are in the pattern at all times. You will be knitting the sole and the rest of the bootie separately, then stitching them together.

4

difficulty level

techniques

Casting on, page 20

Rib stitch, page 29

Garter stitch, page 28

Yarn over, page 32

Increasing, page 30

Picking up stitches, page 37

Joining a new strand of yarn, page 27

Binding off, page 25

Overcast stitch, page 36

Weaving in loose ends, page 26

→

directions

for the top:

1. Loosely cast on 16 stitches.

2. Work 3 rows of knit 2, purl 2 ribbing.

3. Work 6 rows of garter stitch.

4. You will now be creating the beading row for the ribbon to thread through. For this row, knit 1, yarn over, knit 2 together, yarn over. Repeat *knit 2 together, yarn over* across the row until 1 stitch remains. Knit the last stitch. You now have 17 stitches on your needle.

5. You will now begin to divide for the top and sides of the bootie. Knit 6 and place these stitches on stitch holder 1.

6. Knit 5 stitches. Leave them on the needle.

→

you will need

- 1 skein (4 ounces) soft acrylic or wool worsted weight yarn
- 1 pair size 7 needles (to fit newborns; use larger needles for bigger booties)
- 3 stitch holders

Thin ribbon for ankle ties (two 15-inch lengths per pair)

Scissors

Yarn needle

Row counter (optional)

- 2 sewing pins (optional)

7. Place the remaining 6 stitches on stitch holder 2. (Do not knit these stitches yet.)

8. You are now creating the instep. With the 5 stitches on the needle, knit 12 rows of garter stitch. When you are done, place the 5 stitches on stitch holder 3. Cut the yarn, leaving a tail to weave in later.

9. You are now going to knit all the way around the bootie from right to left. Pick up the 6 stitches from holder 2. The tip of your needle should be pointing to the outside of the bootie. Join a strand of yarn (you will have to anchor the loose end with your hand for the first few stitches to prevent it from slipping out) and knit these 6 stitches.

10. With the needle in your left hand, pick up 6 stitches from the side of the instep. Knit these stitches.

11. Slide the 5 stitches from holder 3 onto the free needle. Knit these stitches.

12. Pick up 6 stitches from the other side of the instep and knit them. It may seem awkward as you knit around because the toe will lump up a bit, but don't worry.

13. Slide the 6 stitches from holder 1 onto the free needle. Knit these stitches. You will now have 29 stitches on one needle.

14. Knit 4 more rows of garter stitch, and then bind off loosely.

15. Using the overcast stitch, sew up the back seam. Use the yarn needle to weave in the ends.

for the sole:

1. Cast on 4 stitches for the heel end.

2. Knit 8 rows of garter stitch.

3. Row 9: Knit 2, increase 1 by knitting through the front and back of the stitch, knit 1. You now have 5 stitches on the needle.

4. Row 10: Knit.

5. Row 11: Knit 2, increase 1, knit 2.

6. Row 12: Knit.

7. Row 13: Knit 3, increase 1, knit 2. (You now have 7 stitches on the needle.)

8. Knit 5 more rows of garter stitch (for 18 rows total). Bind off. Leave a long tail at the end to use for attaching the sole to the top.

finishing

Turn the bootie inside out and stitch the sole to the bottom of the bootie with the bind-off tail. You may want to pin the sole at the heel and toe for additional stability. Weave in and trim the ends. Turn the bootie right-side out and weave a 15-inch ribbon (knot the ends to prevent fraying) through the beaded row so the ends are at the front. Tie in a bow.

Now you can make the second bootie!

improvisation ideas: Instead of using ribbon, braid yarn or crochet a chain to make the ankle ties. You can also knit the first 3 ribbed rows in a contrasting color.

tube top

Sure, you could probably buy a tube top for less than $5, but why not choose a lively color and knit one yourself? Working in stretchy elastic yarn on circular needles, you'll create a unique top that's certain to be a summertime hit. It may feel a little strange when you first start knitting with this yarn—just remember to relax and let it ease into place. Resist the urge to pull! The pattern will fit a teen or a petite woman. If you want to knit a larger size, follow the directions in parentheses or increase as described.

3

difficulty level

techniques

Casting on, page 20

Knitting in the round, page 33

Rib stitch, page 29

Joining a new strand of yarn, page 27

Binding off, page 25

Weaving in loose ends, page 26

o o o

you will need

2   balls (50 grams each) stretchy cotton and elastic yarn (98.3% cotton, 1.7% elastic)

1   size 5 circular needle, 24 inches long

1   stitch marker

Tape measure

Scissors

Yarn needle

directions

1.   Cast on 112 *(128)* stitches.

2.   Insert the stitch marker—this will mark the beginning of each new round.

3.   Join the stitches into a circle and work in knit 3, purl 1 ribbing until the top measures 10 *(11)* inches. Note: You will always be starting on the knit 3 part of the pattern when you pass the stitch marker from the left needle to the right.

4.   Bind off loosely. Cut the yarn, leaving a 6-inch tail. Use the yarn needle to weave in the ends.

improvisation idea: Bind off after 6 inches to make a beach-worthy bandeau.

modern-day

accoutrements

change purse

When I taught my cousin Angie to knit, this is what we made. It's quick, easy (all garter stitch except for one yarn over), and makes a great gift. She was so enthused, she immediately made two more for her sisters.

techniques

Casting on, page 20

Garter stitch, page 28

Yarn over, page 32

Binding off, page 25

Overcast stitch, page 36

Weaving in loose ends, page 26

o o o

you will need

1   ball (4 ounces) acrylic or wool worsted weight yarn (or 1 ounce scrap yarn)

1   pair size 8 needles

Tape measure

Scissors

Yarn needle

Sewing needle and thread

Button

directions

1. Cast on 10 stitches.

2. Knit 2 rows of garter stitch.

3. Row 3: Knit 5 stitches, yarn over, and knit the remaining 5 stitches. Now you have 11 stitches. (The yarn over creates the buttonhole.)

4. Keep knitting in garter stitch until the piece measures 5 inches.

5. Bind off, leaving a 10-inch tail.

6. Fold your strip of knitting so that the part with the buttonhole overlaps the rest by an inch. Using the yarn needle, sew up the sides of the purse using the overcast stitch. (You can use the bind-off tail for this.) Weave in and trim the loose ends.

7. Use sewing needle and thread, sew a button on the front of the purse, directly behind where the buttonhole falls.

    improvisation idea: Make your change purse into a child's purse. Braid a 12-inch cord of yarn and attach it to the top of the opening flap, knotting the ends to keep the cord secure and to prevent the braid from unraveling.

cell phone cozy

This is a good project to move on to after the change purse. As you will see, the cell phone cozy is basically the same pattern with three additional increases to shape the flap and an additional yarn over to accommodate the antenna. Why let your cell phone sit around getting dusty or dress it in one of those cheap leather cases when you can knit it up a colorful new suit? Note: This cozy was knit for a cell phone that measures 6 inches tall by 2 1/4 inches wide. You may have to make your cozy a bit shorter and thinner to accommodate a different model.

2

difficulty level

techniques

Casting on, page 20

Garter stitch, page 28

Yarn over, page 32

Increasing, page 30

Binding off, page 25

Overcast stitch, page 36

Weaving in loose ends, page 26

directions

1. Cast on 6 stitches.

2. Knit 3 rows of garter stitch.

3. Row 4: Knit 3 stitches, yarn over, knit the remaining 3 stitches. You now have 7 stitches. (The yarn over creates the buttonhole.)

4. Rows 5 through 7: Knit in garter stitch.

5. Row 8: Knit 1, increase 1 by knitting through the front and back of the next stitch, knit until 1 stitch remains, increase 1. You now have 9 stitches.

6. Rows 9 through 12: Knit in garter stitch.

7. Row 13: Knit 2, yarn over. Knit until 1 stitch remains, increase 1. you now have 11 stitches. (This yarn over creates an opening for your antenna.)

8. Rows 14 through 80: Knit in garter stitch.

9. Bind off, leaving a 24-inch tail.

you will need

1   ball (4 ounces) acrylic or wool
    worsted weight yarn

1   pair size 8 needles

Scissors

Tape measure

Yarn needle

Button

Sewing needle and thread

Row counter (optional)

10. Fold your strip of knitting almost in half so that the antenna hole is located at the top of the cozy and a 2-inch flap with the buttonhole overlaps the rest. Using your yarn needle, sew up the sides of the cozy using the overcast stitch. (You can use your bind-off tail to do this.) Weave in and trim the loose ends.

11. Sew a button on the front of the cozy, directly behind where the buttonhole falls, using your sewing needle and regular thread.

improvisation idea: Make your cozy into an over-the-shoulder carrying case. Braid a 27-inch cord of yarn and attach it to the top of the opening flap, knotting the ends to keep the cord secure and the braid from unraveling.

skiing headband

Knit in very tight knit 1, purl 1 ribbing, this ski headband is guaranteed to keep your ears toasty warm. To make sure it fits snugly, measure around your head where it will go, and then bind off when you have reached 1 inch less than that measurement. (For example, my head measures 21 inches, so I bound off after I reached 20 inches and then sewed the ends together.) The headband will be a little over 3 inches wide, perfect for protecting your ears as you schuss down the slopes.

2

difficulty level

techniques

Casting on, page 20

Rib stitch, page 29

Binding off, page 25

Mattress stitch, page 37

Weaving in loose ends, page 26

o o o

You will need

1   ball (4 ounces) acrylic or wool worsted weight yarn

1   pair size 4 needles

Tape measure

Scissors

Yarn needle

directions

1.   Cast on 17 stitches.

2.   Row 1: Work in knit 1, purl 1 ribbing. (You will end with a knit stitch.)

3.   Row 2: Knit the first stitch, then work in knit 1, purl 1 ribbing until 2 stitches remain on the needle. Knit the last 2 stitches.

4.   Repeat steps 2 and 3 until your headband reaches 20 inches (or your desired length).

5.   Bind off, leaving a 12-inch tail.

6.   Use the yarn needle to sew the two ends together. (You can use your bind-off tail to do this.) Mattress stitch will give you the flattest seam. Weave in and trim the loose ends.

improvisation idea: Make a striped headband by alternating 2 colors every 2 rows. When switching between two colors to make skinny stripes, don't bother to cut the yarn every time you switch. Instead, carry the unused color up the side of your knit piece until it comes into play again, thus avoiding numerous ends to weave in later.

hipster kerchief

Kerchiefs are appropriate headwear almost any time of the year, except when it's freezing cold. In summer, sport one created in cotton. In spring or fall, use a soft wool/silk blend. As you glance over this pattern, you may notice something very interesting. Yes, the kerchief is basically a Company Dishcloth (page 95) without the decrease. See what a difference fancy yarn, larger needles, and a little bit of imagi- nation make!

3

difficulty level

techniques

Casting on, page 20

Garter stitch, page 28

Increasing, page 30

Yarn over, page 32

Binding off, page 25

Weaving in loose ends, page 26

o o o

you will need

1 ball (50 grams) wool/silk blend worsted weight yarn

1 pair size 9 needles

1 pair size 4 needles

Scissors

Yarn needle

directions

for the kerchief:

1. Cast 3 stitches onto the size 9 needles.

2. Row 1: Increase in the first stitch by knitting through the front and back of the stitch, then knit across. (You now have 4 stitches.)

3. Row 2: Increase in the first stitch, then knit across. (You now have 5 stitches.)

4. Row 3: Increase in the first stitch, then knit across. (You now have 6 stitches.)

5. Row 4: Increase in the first stitch, then knit across. (You now have 7 stitches.)

6. Row 5: Increase in the third stitch (for a total of 4 stitches on the right needle), yarn over, and then knit to the end. (You now have 9 stitches.)

7. Row 6: Knit 3 stitches, yarn over, knit to the end.

8. Repeat step 7 until you have 63 stitches on your needle.

9. Knit 4 rows.

10. Bind off. Cut the yarn, and use the yarn needle to weave in the loose ends.

for the ties:

1. Cast 2 stitches onto the size 4 needles.

2. Row 1: Knit 1, purl 1. Repeat this row until the tie measures 6 inches.

3. Bind off.

4. Repeat steps 1 through 3 to knit a second tie.

5. Use the yarn needle to sew the ties to the front corners of the triangle. Weave in and trim the loose ends.

improvisation idea: Want a plainer kerchief without any fussy openwork? Substitute an increase 1 for every yarn over to make a pure garter stitch head covering.

peace, love, and a shoulder bag

Get in touch with your inner flower child by knitting up this laid-back shoulder bag. It's all knit and purl, and the use of short rows in the handle gives it its shape. Because it's worked with a double strand and "knit down" on smaller needles, the bag is too tight to let precious objects slip through the knit.

4

difficulty level

techniques

Casting on, page 20

Garter stitch, page 28

Stockinette stitch, page 28

Binding off, page 25

Weaving in loose ends, page 26

Making seams, page 34

→

directions

for the bag:

1. Using the size 7 needles and with a double strand of yarn, cast on 24 stitches.

2. Rows 1 through 7: Knit.

3. Row 8: Purl.

4. Row 9: Knit.

5. Row 10: Purl.

6. Repeat this 10-row pattern (steps 2 through 5) a total of 11 times. (Feel free to make stripes or blocks of color by alternating 10-row patterns of color.)

7. Knit 7 rows.

8. Bind off.

→

you will need

2 balls (50 grams each) acrylic
or wool worsted weight yarn for
the body of the bag

2 balls (50 grams each) acrylic
or wool worsted weight yarn
for the shoulder strap

1 pair size 7 needles

1 size 8 circular needle,
29 inches or longer

Scissors

Yarn needle

Sewing pins

Row counter (optional)

for the shoulder strap:

You will be casting on the length of the strap and then knitting back and forth in short and regular rows to shape it.

1. Using the size 8 circular needle and with a double strand of yarn, cast on 110 stitches.

2. Row 1 (short row): Knit 20 stitches and turn your work.

3. Row 2 (short row): Knit 20 stitches back.

4. Row 3: Knit all 110 stitches. You will be back at the side you started on.

5. Row 4 (short row): Knit 20 stitches and turn your work.

6. Row 5 (short row): Knit 20 stitches back.

7. Row 6: Knit all 110 stitches.

8. Row 7 (short row): Knit 20 stitches and turn your work.

9. Row 8 (short row): Knit 20 stitches back.

10. Row 9: Knit all 110 stitches.

11. Row 10 (short row): Knit 20 stitches and turn your work.

12. Row 11 (short row): Knit 20 stitches back.

13. Bind off.

14. Weave in and trim the loose ends.

finishing

Turn the bag and the handle wrong-side out, match the bottom part of the strap to the base of the bag, and pin in place. Use the mattress stitch or the overcast stitch to sew together.

improvisation idea: Use metallic yarn to change your "earth mother" bag into an evening bag.

creative home
decor ○ ○ ○

the simple square

You might think of squares as yawn-inducing quadrilaterals, but think of all the happening things they can be used to make! You can create coasters, placemats, table runners, festive bibs, baby blankets, bed-size blankets—you name it. And by varying the pattern square by square, you can build up an impressive repertoire of stitches. Just remember to check the gauge when you switch stitches and yarn; it's difficult to piece together a bunch of dissimilarly sized squares. To illustrate this, I've knitted up 9 different squares. They are all made from worsted weight yarn and have a cast-on row of 20 stitches. Can you believe it?

1-3

difficulty level

techniques

Casting on, page 20

Garter, rib, or seed stitch, pages 28–29

Binding off, page 25

Making seams, page 34

Weaving in loose ends, page 26

o o o

you will need

Yarn that you like

Appropriate size needles

Tape measure (optional)

Scissors

Yarn needle

Row counter (optional)

Gauge aid (optional)

directions

1. For each square: Cast on your chosen number of stitches.

2. You will be working each square in your chosen stitch. (Or stitches! Feel free to mix and match, to see what the yarn can do.) Knit until you have a square that is as high as it is wide. You can determine this by measuring with a tape measure or by folding the square in half diagonally to create 2 equal triangles.

3. Bind off.

4. Repeat steps 1 through 3 until you have as many completed squares as you need.

5. Arrange the squares in an attractive and interesting pattern, and sew them together using any of the 3 stitches in the "Making Seams" section. (Unless they're coasters—in that case, scatter them around!)

improvisation idea: Make a nouveau rag rug using squares of heavier cotton yarn.

petite pillow cover

Remember how I said gauge isn't always that important? Well, for this project it is, and unless your pillow form size and knitting gauge are exactly the same as mine (or unless you decide to stuff your pillow with polyester fiber), you will want to make some calculations to ensure that your cover will fit. This cover is made of 2 squares that are sewn together. As a rule, you need to add ¼ inch on all sides to allow for seams, so since my form is 12 inches square, I wanted to knit two 12½-by-12½-inch squares. I knit a swatch with size 10½ needles and found that my gauge was 2½ stitches per inch and 4 rows per inch. This meant that I needed to cast on 32 stitches (12.5 x 2.5 is 31.25, so I rounded up) to reach 12½ inches in width, and then knit for 50 (12.5 x 4) rows to reach 12½ inches in length. Voilà! There's the pattern. This formula is easily adapted to fit any size pillow form.

2

difficulty level

techniques

Gauge, page 38

Casting on, page 20

Stockinette stitch, page 28

Binding off, page 25

Making seams, page 34

Weaving in loose ends, page 26

→

directions

1. Make a swatch and check your gauge. If it is not 2½ stitches per inch and 4 rows per inch, change your needle size to match it (or recalculate the stitches and rows, as described above).

2. Cast on 32 stitches.

3. Knit 50 rows in stockinette stitch.

4. Bind off.

5. Repeat steps 2 through 4 to make a second square exactly the same size as the first. (Repeat step 1 if you're switching yarns for the second side.)

6. Match up the finished squares. The right sides should be on the inside at this point. You may want to pin the squares in place so they don't slip as you sew around.

→

you will need

2 skeins (4 ounces each) bulky acrylic yarn

1 pair size 10½ needles

1 pillow form (12 inches square) or a bag of polyester fiber filling

Scissors

Sewing pins

Yarn needle

Gauge aid (optional)

Row counter (optional)

7. Using your yarn needle and extra yarn, sew up 3 sides of the cover, using any of the 3 stitches in the "Making Seams" section. This is a great opportunity to experiment and find the one you like best. Weave in and trim the loose ends.

8. Turn the cover right-side out and insert the pillow form.

9. Pin the top edges of the pillow together and sew up the final side, being careful to make the stitches as invisible as possible. When you reach the end, weave in and trim the tail.

improvisation idea: Change colors after every 2 rows for a sophisticated stripe. You don't need to cut the yarn—just carry it up the side. You can still leave the other side of the pillow solid and flip it over for a change of scene.

company dishcloth

Basic dishcloths are great, but there may be times when you long for something a little fancier. Perhaps you want to present a dishcloth as a gift or impress that VIP who's coming to dinner. In that case, whip up one of these and show it off. As an added bonus, creating this dishcloth will also give you invaluable practice increasing and decreasing, as it is knit from one corner to the other.

3

difficulty level

techniques

Casting on, page 20

Garter stitch, page 28

Increasing, page 30

Yarn over, page 32

Decreasing, page 31

Binding off, page 25

Weaving in loose ends, page 26

o o o

you will need

1   ball (2 ounces) 100% cotton worsted weight yarn

1   pair size 7 needles

Scissors

Yarn needle

Row counter (optional)

directions

1. Cast on 4 stitches.

2. Row 1: Increase in the first stitch by knitting through the front and back of the stitch, then knit across. (You now have 5 stitches.)

3. Row 2: Increase in the first stitch, then knit across. (You now have 6 stitches.)

4. Row 3: Increase in the first stitch, then knit across. (You now have 7 stitches.)

5. Row 4: Increase in the third stitch (for a total of 4 stitches on the right needle), yarn over, and then knit to the end. (You now have 9 stitches.)

6. Row 5: Knit 3 stitches, yarn over, and knit to the end.

7. Repeat step 6 until you have 50 stitches on your needle.

8. You will now begin to decrease. Knit 2, knit 2 together, yarn over, knit 2 together, and then knit to the end. Repeat this pattern until you have 8 stitches on your needle.

9. Decrease to 4 stitches by knitting 2 stitches together across the entire row.

10. Bind off. Cut the yarn and use the yarn needle to weave in the loose ends.

improvisation idea: Make a jumbo dishcloth by increasing the number of stitches to 60 before you start to decrease.

beer cozy

Okay, so it doesn't exactly help keep the beer cold. However, it does keep your hand warm and, more importantly, it looks great. This is a fabulous gift for the beer drinkers in your life. It also provides a great introduction to knitting in the round using double-pointed needles. If you can make this cozy, you are ready to move on to mittens.

3

difficulty level

techniques

Casting on, page 20

Knitting in the round, page 33

Rib stitch, page 29

Stockinette stitch, page 28

Binding off, page 25

Weaving in loose ends, page 26

o o o

you will need

1   ball (100 grams) acrylic worsted weight yarn, or 2 colors of scrap yarn 1 ounce each) for a striped cozy

4   size 6 double-pointed needles

Scissors

Yarn needle

Row counter (optional)

directions

1. Cast 32 stitches onto 1 of the needles. Divide the stitches among 3 of the needles, with 12, 12, and 8 stitches on the needles.

2. Join the stitches in a circle and work 5 rounds in knit 2, purl 2 ribbing.

3. Work the next 14 rounds in stockinette stitch (knit only, since you're working in the round). If you want to make a stripe around the cozy, attach the second color at the beginning of round 9 and return to the main color at the beginning of round 17.

4. Work 5 rounds in knit 2, purl 2 ribbing.

5. Bind off, and use your yarn needle to weave in the loose ends.

    improvisation ideas: Knit the cozy in your favorite team's colors. You can also personalize it by cross-stitching an initial on the front.

paperweight

Do you have an unclothed rock holding down papers on your desk? Well, slip that puppy into a spectacular sheath and raise the tone of the entire office. I recommend using mohair for the ultimate contrast between soft and hard. It is also fine enough to avoid lumps when you sew the ends together. This project is a good way to explore what gauge means (no two rocks will be the same size, so you have to figure it out) and to see how understanding gauge can help you become a more creative knitter. It will also give you experience working with mohair, a beautiful, soft yarn that can be tricky to knit. It's good to try a small project like this before committing to that fabulous mohair sweater.

3

difficulty level

techniques

Gauge, page 38

Casting on, page 20

Knitting in the round, page 33

Stockinette stitch, page 28

Binding off, page 25

Weaving in loose ends, page 26

→

directions

1. With your tape measure, measure the circumference of your rock at its thickest point and its height from bottom to top. You will basically be fitting it for a sweater. Write down these measurements. (My rock was 8 inches around at its thickest point and stood 5 inches tall.)

2. Make a swatch and check your gauge. (My swatch measured 3 stitches per inch across and 5 rows per inch, knit on size 9 needles.) Now figure out how many stitches to cast on and how many rows to knit by plugging in your measurements. For example, my rock was 8 inches in circumference at its thickest point and 5 inches tall. I needed to make sure my paperweight cover was 8 inches wide to fit around the rock. Because my gauge was 3 stitches per inch across, I multiplied 3 stitches times 8 inches and cast on 24 stitches. To make sure the cover was long enough, I needed to knit 5 inches of fabric to cover the rock from bottom to top. I could have measured this by eye, but I was scientific and multiplied 5 rows per inch by 5 inches tall and found that I needed 25 rows.

    →

you will need

1   ball (50 grams) mohair (this will cover **a lot** of paper-weights)

4   size 9 double-pointed needles

Tape measure

1   or more rocks, preferably rounded

Scissors

Yarn needle

Gauge aid (optional)

Row counter (optional)

3. Cast the appropriate number of stitches on 1 of your double-pointed needles leaving an 8-inch tail. Divide the stitches among 3 of the needles.

4. Join the stitches into a circle and work in stockinette stitch until you reach the appropriate length.

5. Cut the yarn, leaving an 8-inch tail. Use the yarn needle to thread the tail through the remaining stitches. Pull it tight and weave in the end.

6. Slip the cover over your rock. Use the cast-on tail of yarn to sew this end of the cover together. Because you are working with mohair, it will be satisfyingly unlumpy. When it is closed to your satisfaction, weave in and trim the end.

improvisation idea: Knit a striped cover for your rock by changing yarn every 2 rows.

groovy curtain

Like others in my neighborhood, I generally don't believe in curtains. But I had to make
an exception for one very thin window that looks out onto someone else's window. Use
a loose garter stitch to make a pseudo-barrier between yourself and the outside world.
It's easy to color-coordinate with your decor, and it provides that illusion of being in
your own space. And since it is knit in vertical stripes, once you get started it's easy to
gauge how many rows you should knit—just keep holding it up to the window until it fits.

3

difficulty level

techniques

Casting on, page 20

Garter stitch, page 28

Joining a new strand of yarn,
page 27

Binding off, page 25

Weaving in loose ends, page 26

Fringe, page 32

→

directions

1. Measure your window. Decide where your curtain rod will hang and
    where you want the bottom of the curtain to fall. Remember that you
    will need 2 extra inches to make the curtain rod pocket at the end. Do
    you want to add 6 inches of fringe that sweeps the bottom sill (and
    maybe hides some dust)? Take all of this into consideration before you
    start knitting.

2. Cast on 50 stitches with wool worsted, which we will now call yarn 1.
    (You will need to cast on more for a taller window and less for a shorter
    one. It's difficult to figure out gauge with the blend of chunky and thin
    yarn, so the best way to determine the number of stitches to cast on is to
    make an educated guess and then check the knit material after about 6
    rows. You can also adjust the fringe later to make the curtain fit.)

3. Row 1: Knit using yarn 1.

4. Rows 2 and 3: Knit using chunky slub, which we'll call yarn 2.

5. Rows 4 and 5: Knit using cotton worsted, yarn 3.

6. Rows 6 and 7: Knit using yarn 1.

    →

you will need

1   ball (4 ounces) wool worsted
    weight yarn

1   ball (5 ounces) chunky slub (a
    thick-and-thin yarn that looks
    like bouclé gone wild) or heavy
    cotton chenille

1   ball (4 ounces) cotton worsted
    weight yarn

1   size 15 circular needle,
    29 inches or longer

Tape measure

Scissors

Yarn needle

7. Repeat steps 4 through 6, alternating yarns every 2 rows, until the curtain reaches the desired width. (The pattern was repeated a total of 9 times for the sample curtain.)

8. Bind off. Weave in and trim the loose ends.

9. Fold 2 inches of fabric at the top of the curtain over. Using the yarn needle and extra worsted weight yarn, stitch along the bottom to form the rod pocket.

10. Make the fringe. One slub fringe for every 4 rows of worsted works well.

note: The sample curtain was made to cover a 12-by-32-inch window. The knit fabric measured 31 by 11 inches when done, then 2 inches of the 31 inches were folded over and sewn to create the rod pocket. I added 6 inches of fringe, so the finished curtain measured 35 inches from rod to sill.

improvisation idea: A wider, longer curtain would make a very vivacious lap throw or shawl. You could also mix super-thin yarns with big needles to make a net-like curtain.

poncho

Admit it. Either you wore one as a child or you secretly coveted one. Now's your chance to make up for lost time. This swinging cover-up is guaranteed to warm the heart and delight the eye, and best of all, it's easy to create! Just knit two 15-by-30-inch rectangles with a double strand of yarn, and join. It's a classic sixties-style pattern.

3

difficulty level

techniques

Gauge, page 38

Casting on, page 20

Seed stitch, page 29

Joining a new strand of yarn, page 27

Binding off, page 25

Overcast stitch, page 36

Weaving in loose ends, page 26

Fringe, page 32

→

directions

1. Working with a double strand of yarn, make a seed stitch swatch and check your gauge. If it is not 2½ stitches per inch across, change your needle size to match it.

2. Cast on 35 stitches, with a double strand of yarn.

3. Knit in seed stitch until the piece is 30 inches long.

4. Bind off, leaving about a 6-inch tail.

5. Repeat steps 2 through 4 to make a second rectangle that is exactly the same size as the first.

→

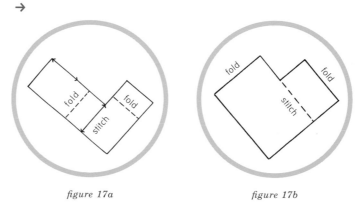

figure 17a   figure 17b

you will need

6 skeins (4 ounces each) acrylic or wool worsted weight yarn

1 size 10½ circular needle, 24 inches long

Tape measure

Scissors

Yarn needle

Sewing pins (optional)

Gauge aid (optional)

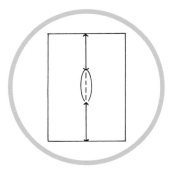

figure 18

6. Match up the finished rectangles, as shown in figure 17a. Fold as shown and sew together, using the overcast stitch. You will end up with the shape shown in figure 17b.

7. Weave in and trim the loose ends.

8. Add fringe, if desired. The fringe in the photo was placed every third row, but you may want to place it every second row for a denser look.

improvisation idea: To make a boxier poncho, knit two 15-by-50-inch rectangles, and sew them together side by side as shown in figure 18. Make sure you leave at least a 10-inch opening in the center for your head. Who says you have to stitch your poncho together using the same color yarn you used to make it? Stitching, say, a navy blue poncho together with off-white yarn creates an interesting and eye-catching effect.

urban folk shawl

The openwork pattern and choice of esoteric yarn make this one of our more difficult projects. But it's worth it when you can sing along to Fleetwood Mac in style.

4

difficulty level

techniques

Casting on, page 20

Garter stitch, page 28

Joining a new strand of yarn, page 27

Yarn over, page 32

Binding off, page 25

Fringe, page 32

○ ○ ○

you will need

5   different colors of yarn:

   2   skeins (4 ounces each) bulky wool yarn

   2   skeins (50 grams each) mohair

   1   skein (100 grams) wool worsted weight yarn

   2   skeins (50 grams each) cotton worsted weight yarn

   1   skein (50 grams) soft, wool sport or fingering weight yarn

1   size 9 circular needle, 24 inches long

Scissors, tape measure, yarn needle

directions

1. Cast on 170 stitches with bulky weight wool.

2. Row 1: Knit. Cut the yarn, leaving an 8-inch end for fringe.

3. Row 2: Change color. Attach the new yarn, leaving an 8-inch end. Knit 1, yarn over, knit 2 together, yarn over. Work across the row, repeating *knit 2 together, yarn over* until there are 3 stitches left on your needle. End the row with knit 2 together, knit 1.

4. Row 3: Knit.

5. Repeat steps 3 and 4 until you have 90 rows total.

6. Bind off.

7. Cut 16-inch lengths of yarn (1 for every 2 rows), and add fringe to the opposite side.

improvisation idea: Channel the shawl through your favorite retro rock star. What would Janis Joplin have liked?

simple sweater

Because this sweater is knit in the round from the top down, you won't have to worry about seams, and you can make some adjustments as you go. The pattern is for a woman's size small. If you want to knit a medium or large, follow the directions in parentheses.

5

difficulty level

techniques

Gauge, page 38

Casting on, page 20

Knitting in the round, page 33

Rib stitch, page 29

Stockinette stitch, page 28

Increasing, page 30

Decreasing, page 31

Joining a new strand of yarn, page 27

Picking up stitches, page 37

Binding off, page 25

Weaving in loose ends, page 26

Blocking, page 40

directions

for the sweater body:

1. Make a stockinette stitch swatch with size 13 needles, and check your gauge. If it is not 2½ stitches per inch across, change your needle size.

2. Neck: Cast 40 *(42, 44)* stitches onto the 16-inch size 11 needle. Place a color A marker on the needle. Join and work 4 rounds in knit-1, purl-1 ribbing.

3. Shoulders: Switch to the 29-inch size 13 needle, and work 1 round, knitting all stitches. Round 1 (increase round): Beginning just after the color A marker, increase 1 by knitting through the front and back of the stitch, knit 13 *(14, 14)*, increase 1 and place a color B marker on the needle (this is the front of the sweater). Increase 1, knit 3 *(3, 4)*, increase 1 and place another color B marker (this is a sleeve). Increase 1, knit 13 *(14, 14)*, increase 1 and place the third color B marker (this is the back). Increase 1, knit 3 *(3, 4)*, increase 1 (the second sleeve). You now have 48 *(50, 52)* stitches on your needle. Round 2: Knit all stitches.

4. Continue to alternate increase rounds with straight knit rounds 12 more times. In every increase round, increase before and after each color marker, for a total of 8 additional stitches every time you repeat round 1. You may want to count stitches when you work round 2 to make sure you're on track. You are finished shaping the shoulders when you have a total of 136 *(146, 164)* stitches on your needle. Knit one more round.

→

6 skeins (100 grams each) wool
   or acrylic bulky yarn (7, 9)

1 size 13 circular needle
   29 inches long

1 size 11 circular needle
   29 inches long

1 size 13 circular needle
   16 inches long

1 size 11 circular needle
   16 inches long

2 stitch holders

Stitch markers: 1 of color A and
3 of color B

Tape measure

Scissors

Yarn needle

Gauge aid (optional)

5. Setting aside the sleeve stitches: Starting from A color marker, knit 39 *(42, 46)* stitches across the front to the first B color marker. Put next 29 *(31, 36)* stitches onto stitch holder. This is your first sleeve. Turn your work so the wrong side faces you and cast on 2 *(3, 4)* underarm stitches. Turn work so right side faces you, and knit across next 39 *(42, 46)* stitches. Put next 29 *(31, 36)* stitches onto a stitch holder. Again, cast on 2 *(3, 4)* stitches.

6. Body: Insert marker. Join and continue knitting the 82 *(90, 100)* stitches until piece measures 14 *(16, 18)* inches from underarm.

7. Bottom ribbing: Switch to the 29-inch size 11 needle and work two rounds in knit 1, purl 1 ribbing. Bind off.

for the sleeves:

1. Transfer 29 *(31, 36)* stitches from stitch holder onto the 16-inch size 13 circular needle. Pick up 5 *(5, 6)* stitches from underarm. Insert marker at center of underarm. You will be knitting all stitches.

2. Attach a new ball of yarn and join. Rounds 1 and 2: Knit all stitches. Round 3: (decrease round). Knit two together, then knit until end of round.

3. Repeat step 2 until 20 *(22, 26)* stitches remain. Knit 1 *(3, 1)* more round(s).

4. Switch to the 16-inch size 11 needle. Work two rounds in knit-1, purl-1 ribbing. Bind off.

5. Repeat steps 1 through 4 to knit the second sleeve.

finishing:

Use the yarn needle to weave in the loose ends. Block your sweater, if desired.

improvisation idea: Add a nice broad stripe in the middle if you are averse to solid colors.

daring halter

This cool cotton halter is perfect for those days when it's just too hot for a T-shirt. Since you will be working with a double strand of yarn in two different colors, the halter knits up quickly and is a unique creation. Make it before the next heat wave strikes! The directions make a small halter. If you want to knit a medium one, follow the directions in parentheses.

3

difficulty level

techniques

Gauge, page 38

Casting on, page 20

Rib stitch, page 29

Stockinette stitch, page 28

Decreasing, page 31

Garter stitch, page 28

Joining a new strand of yarn, page 27

Picking up stitches, page 37

Binding off, page 25

Weaving in loose ends, page 26

→

directions

1. Working with a double strand of yarn, make a stockinette stitch swatch with size 9 needles, and check your gauge. If it is not 3½ stitches per inch across, change your needle size to match it.

2. Cast 54 *(60)* stitches onto the size 9 circular needle. Work in knit 2, purl 2 ribbing until the piece measures 2 *(3)* inches.

3. Knit in stockinette stitch for 2 inches. Your entire piece should measure 4 *(5)* inches. You will now begin to decrease.

4. Row 1: Knit 1, knit 2 together, knit until 3 stitches remain on your needle, slip 1, knit 1, pass slipped stitch over, knit last stitch. Row 2: Purl. Repeat these 2 rows 19 times until 16 *(20)* stitches remain on the needles. You will decrease 2 stitches every time you repeat row 1.

5. Bind off.

6. Make the 4 halter ties by using size 7 needles to pick up 3 stitches *per tie* from the edges of the halter (figure 19). Knit each tie in garter stitch, using a single strand of yarn, until it is 11 inches long.

7. Weave in and trim the loose ends.

→

you will need

4 skeins (50 grams each)
   cotton/acrylic blend worsted
   weight yarn

1 size 9 circular needle,
   24 inches long

1 pair size 7 needles (straight
   or circular)

Tape measure

Scissors

Yarn needle

Gauge aid (optional)

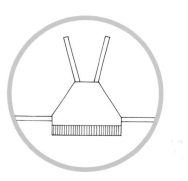

figure 19

improvisation idea: As you can see, knitting double with 2 different colors of yarns produces a visually interesting, unique pattern. You might want to experiment further with this on your own, adapting simpler recipes you may have tried before like "Plain Old Scarf." (You might want to move up a bit with needle size for a looser weave.) On the other hand, you may prefer a nice, solid halter. In that case, by all means, use two same colors skeins!

resources

yarn shops

There's nothing like being able to touch and see yarn. That's why it is important to find out where your local yarn shop is and pay a visit. Unfortunately, not everyone lives near a nice one. The best place in your area may be a department store that carries only acrylic, while you want to work with wool. Don't despair: Thanks to the magic of the Internet you can have a virtual yarn store in your very own home.

From Artfibers in San Francisco (www.artfibers.com) to Halcyon Yarn in Bath, Maine (www.halcyonyarn.com), the United States is chock-full of knitting stores, and you are certain to find one that's just right for you. You can find some of the yarns used in *Knitting Pretty* at www.pinetreeyarns.com and www.peacefleece.com.

books

Visit your local library to see what kind of knitting selection they have. The books listed below are good for beginners.

- *Big Book of Knitting* by Katharina Buss (Sterling Publications, 2001).

- *Kids Knitting* by Melanie Falick (Artisan, 1998).

- *Knitting Without Tears* by Elizabeth Zimmermann (Simon & Schuster, 1973).

- *Vogue Knitting: The Ultimate Knitting Book* by *Vogue Knitting* magazine (Pantheon Books, 1989).

magazines

- *Bust*. This saucy New York–based magazine occasionally includes out-of-sight patterns (the bikini was a classic) and often features craft-friendly articles. For more information, visit www.bust.com.

- *Rebecca*. You can find this German pattern magazine (which is chock-full of exciting designs aimed at the younger set) in better yarn stores. Don't worry— English translations are provided on a photocopied insert. Their Web site is at www.rebecca-online.de, but it is available only in German.

- *Rowan*. A British pattern magazine that not only has superb designs but also has features on techniques, fibers, and knitwear designers. Again, you will find it in yarn stores or on the Web at www.rowanyarns.co.uk.

miscellaneous

- Ask relatives or elderly friends if they have any knitting books or patterns you could borrow or have. A brief visit to the attic will sometimes yield a wealth of treasures.

- Visit garage sales or thrift stores for patterns, books, and maybe even extra yarn and needles.

- Visit the Internet for patterns and advice. One of my favorite sites is www.yesterknits.com, which boasts the largest collection of vintage knitting patterns in the world.

- Search out vintage magazines, like *Ladies' Home Journal, Needlecraft, American Home,* and *McCall's Needlework*. You may be able to find these at garage sales, antique shops, and thrift stores, or in someone's attic.

social opportunities

You don't have to knit alone if you don't want to! Here are some suggestions.

- Take classes at your local yarn shop.

- Join a knitting group. The Knitting Guild of America has many chapters. Find the one nearest you at www.tkga.com.

- Start your own knitting group with a few friends.

- Attend a Knit-Out, sponsored by the Craft Yarn Council. Knit-Outs take place in September and are forums for sharing finished projects, learning new stitches, and getting free patterns and advice. For more information on the next one near you, visit www.craftyarncouncil.com/knitoutbrochure.html.

- Knit for charity. Visit www.tkga.com/links.htm for information about Warm Up America and other organizations.

- Knit in public. Knitters and nonknitters often will want to chat about their experiences and the project you're working on. It's a welcome touch of small-town living in an increasingly urban existence.

knitting abbreviations

abbreviation	meaning
alt	alternate
beg	beginning
bl	block
BO	bind off
CC	contrasting color
dble	double
dec	decrease
dp	double-pointed needle
foll	following
gm	gram
inc	increase
k	knit
lp(s)	loop(s)
MC	main color
oz	ounce
p	purl
patt	pattern
psso	pass slipped stitch over
rem	remaining
rep	repeat
RS	right side
rnd(s)	round(s)
sk	skip

abbreviation	meaning
sl	slip
sl st	slip stitch
ssk	slip, slip, knit
st(s)	stitch(es)
st st	stockinette stitch
tog	together
WS	wrong side
yo	yarn over

symbol	meaning
* *	repeat what is between the asterisks a specified number of times
( )	repeat what is between the parentheses as many times as specified

some helpful terms

yarn double	use 2 strands of yarn simultaneously
work even	continue in the same stitch pattern, with no increases or decreases, until further directed

yarns used for projects

first projects

bookmark

Peace fleece, worsted weight, 30% mohair, 70% wool, 4-ounce skein.
Colors: Patience Blue, Volgassippi Blue, Latvian Lavender

plain old scarf

Chianti, worsted weight, 100% wool, 50 gram skein.
Colors: #16, #172

dishcloth

Lily's Sugar 'n Cream, worsted weight 100% cotton, 2-ounce skein.
Colors: Teal Ombre, Light Green

o o o

old favorites

ice-skating scarf

Koigu, Fancy Merino, Bouclé, 100% merino wool, 50-gram skein.
Color: #F448, Classic Elite, Montera 50% llama, 50% wool, 100-gram skein.
Color: Andes Lavender

super-long ribbed scarf

Lamb's Pride, bulky, 85% wool, 15% mohair, 4-ounce skein (113 grams).
Color: Limeade

comfy ribbed hat

Lamb's Pride, bulky 85% wool, 15% mohair, 4-ounce skein (113 grams).
Color: Sable

sculpted hat

Peace fleece, worsted weight, 30% mohair, 70% wool, 4-ounce skein.
Colors: Ukrainian Red, Perestroika Pink, Moscow Magic Pink

roll-up hat

Bartlett Yarns, worsted weight 100% wool 4-ounce skein.
Color: Coral Heather

warmest mittens

Peace fleece, worsted weight, 30% mohair, 70% wool, 4-ounce skein.
Colors: Volgassippi Blue, Violet Vyehchyeerom, Patience Blue

slippers

Lamb's Pride, bulky, 85% wool, 15% mohair, 4-ounce skein (113 grams).
Color: Fuchsia

o o o

adorable knits for kids of all ages

wiggly worm scarf

Manos del Uruguay, worsted weight, handspun pure wool, kettle dyed, 100-gram skein.
Color: #54

sock puppet couture

various yarns

sky blue baby blanket

Manos del Uruguay, worsted weight, handspun pure wool, kettle dyed, 100-gram skein.
Colors: #6, #20, #38, #63, #82, A, W

cute as can be baby booties

Peace fleece, worsted weight, 85% wool, 15% mohair, 4-ounce skein.
Color: Latvian Lavender

tube top

Cascade Yarns "Fixation" 98.3% cotton, 1.7% elastic, 50-gram skein.
Color: #9442

o o o

modern-day accoutrements

change purse

Peace fleece, worsted weight, 30% mohair, 70% wool, 4-ounce skein.
Color: Blueberry Borscht

cell phone cozy

Peace fleece, worsted weight, 30% mohair, 70% wool, 4-ounce skein.
Color: Georgia Rose

skiing headband

Peace fleece, worsted weight, 30% mohair, 70% wool, 4-ounce skein.
Colors: Firebird Orange, Ukrainian Red

hipster kerchief

Noro "Silk Garden," 45% silk, 45% kid mohair, 10% lamb's wool, 50-gram skein.
Color: #8

peace, love, and a shoulder bag

Nemo, extra-fine merino, 100% wool, 50-gram skein.
Colors: #4, #13

o o o

creative home decor

the simple square

various yarns

petite pillow cover

tma yarns "Quick 'n Easy Chunky," 100% acrylic, 5-ounce skein.
Colors: Purple Passion, Country Blue

company dishcloth

Lily's Sugar 'n Cream, worsted weight, 100% cotton yarn, 2-ounce skein.
Colors: Shaded Denim, Light Blue

beer cozy

Red Heart, worsted weight, 100% acrylic, 100-gram skein.
Colors: #0738 and #336

paperweight

Katia Ingenua 78% mohair, 13% nylon, 9% wool, 50-gram skein.
Colors: #17, #18, #20

groovy curtain

Pine Tree Yarns "Mikado," 96% wool, 4% nylon, 8-ounce skein (156 yards).
Pine Tree Yarns "Mackensie," 70% wool, 30% silk, 4-ounce skein (176 yards).
Pine Tree Yarns' "Cotton Comfort," 80% wool, 20% cotton, 2-ounce skein (180 yards).
Color: Wild Berries

o o o

tops of all types

urban folk shawl

Missions Falls "1824 Cotton" 100% cotton, 50-gram skein.
Color: #403
Classic Elite "La Gran Mohair," 76.5% mohair, 17.5% wool, 6% nylon 42-gram skein.
Colors: #4, #06579, #1399,
Rowan "Kid Classic," 70% lambswool, 26% kid mohair, 4% nylon, 50-gram skein.
Color: #824
Manos del Uruguay, worsted weight, pure wool 100-gram skein.
Color: #63
Peace Fleece, worsted weight, 30% mohair, 70% wool, 4-ounce skein.
Color: Latvian Lavender

poncho

Peace fleece, worsted weight, 30% mohair, 70% wool, 4-ounce skein.
Color: Siberian Midnight
Fringe: Siberian Midnight, Galooboy Blue

simple sweater

Reynolds "Bulky Lopi," 100% virgin wool, 100-gram skein.
Color: #0604

daring halter

Rowan "All Seasons Cotton," 60% cotton, 40% acrylic, 50-gram skein.
Colors: #197, #185

o o o

index

tops
of all types